A Question
of Order
India, Turkey,
and the Return of
Strongmen

COLUMBIA GLOBAL REPORTS
NEW YORK

of Order
India, Turkey,
and the Return of
Strongmen

Basharat Peer

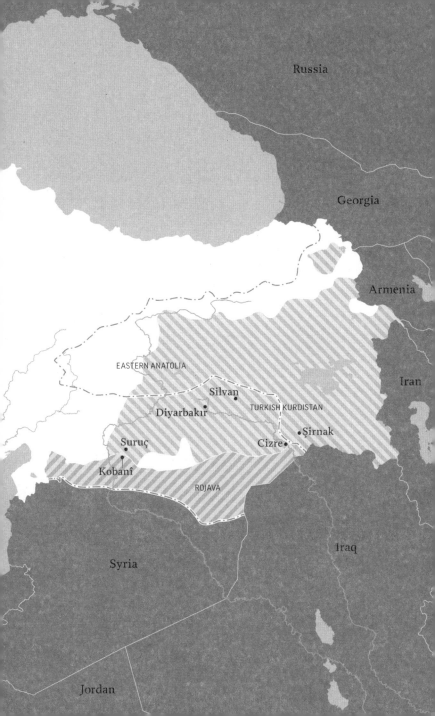

Published by Columbia Global Reports
91 Claremont Avenue, Suite 515
New York, NY 10027
globalreports.columbia.edu
facebook.com/columbiaglobalreports
@columbiaGR

Library of Congress Control Number:
2016945883
ISBN: 978-0997126426

Book design by Strick&Williams
Map design by Jeffrey L. Ward
Author photograph by Miranda Sita

Printed in the United States of America

A Question
of Order
India, Turkey,
and the Return of
Strongmen

CONTENTS

Prologue

Everyone's experience with democracy is different.

I grew up in the Indian-controlled part of the disputed region of Kashmir. India's vaunted democracy seemed to stop short of the mountains circling my hometown as the government eroded the region's autonomous status, empowered mimic men, and ruthlessly crushed dissent. The infamously rigged 1987 elections and a legacy of arresting and torturing activists from the opposition led to rebellion in the winter of 1989–90. A brutal cycle of insurgency and counter-insurgency, which has claimed more than 70,000 lives since, turned Kashmir into the most militarized zone in the world. Indian soldiers were given immunity from prosecution even if they killed unarmed, innocent Kashmiri civilians. In a recent flareup in July 2016, Indian troops fired pellet guns at the eyes of Kashmiri protesters and blinded or partially blinded around

700 teenagers and young men. Not a single man who fired those
guns will be prosecuted in a court of law.

The cliché about India is that it is "the world's largest democracy." Numerical strength seems to magically imbue the country with liberal traditions and equality for its populace. By frequently repeating the description, secular and religious nationalists overlook gross inequalities between rich and poor, mistreatment of ethnic and religious minorities, segregation in cities, everyday violence against lower castes, brutal campaigns of pacification in Kashmir, and rebellions in northeastern states near the China, Bangladesh, and Myanmar borders.

The periphery might be ignored but it has a way of intruding upon the center. A nation's illiberal practices on its borders do not remain isolated there. Using militant nationalism to beat up on peripheral populations often paves way for the rise of authoritarian figures in the center. The obliteration of Grozny contributed to the reign of Russian strongman Vladimir Putin. Putin's return to the Kremlin as president in May 2012 and his subsequent decimation of oppositional forces is one of the more striking markers of the rise of illiberal regimes led by strongmen in the post-Cold War world.

After the collapse of the Soviet Union, the West expected an international order of liberal democracy and free markets to be the dominant paradigm for the world, but this did not materialize. There might be fewer traditional dictatorships across the globe in the twenty-first century, but the world is increasingly dominated by governments that are both democratic and authoritarian on the same afternoon. This is the age of hybrid regimes.

14   The political scientist Javier Corrales, while describing Hugo Chavez's Venezuela, has defined a hybrid regime as "one in which the executive branch concentrates powers to the detriment of nonstate and opposition actors." At the heart of this crisis is the rise of "illiberal democracy," in Fareed Zakaria's famous phrase. "Across the globe, democratically elected regimes, often ones that have been reelected or reaffirmed through referenda, are routinely ignoring constitutional limits on their power and denying their citizens of basic rights," Zakaria wrote in a classic 1997 essay in *Foreign Affairs*.

The importance of civil liberties and protections from the tyranny of the majority are the two great promises of liberal democracy. Those two values are in recession in the current political moment. And an increasing number of illiberal democracies are unabashedly being led by undemocratic, aggressive strongmen. Popular electoral support for leaders such as Russia's Vladimir Putin, Turkey's Recep Tayyip Erdoğan, India's Narendra Modi, Egypt's Abdel Fattah el-Sisi, Hungary's Victor Orbán, Chad's Idriss Déby, Belarus's Alexander Lukashenko, Cambodia's Hun Sen, and Singapore's Lee Hsien Loong, just to name a few, has created a new class of elected autocrats who have pushed back liberal democratic practices. These strongmen have won electoral mandates from voters motivated by religious and ethnic nationalism, economic anxieties, and disillusionment with earlier weak, inefficient, or corrupt elites.

The modern strongmen share a certain set of qualities. They embrace militant nationalism, exude an aura of personal menace and strength, persecute political opponents, and seek to control media coverage. They have little patience for criticism

and despise civil society. They have a certain love for efficiency   15
and disregard for cumbersome democratic processes.

Strongmen are revisionists who share a preference for rewriting school textbooks, retelling tales of ancient glories, and reviving old wounds. They are united by their promises to make their countries great again. And they master the art of converting the fears and insecurities of citizens into electoral support. They position themselves as saviors on white horses, big-chested men who alone can rescue their nations from peril. "Illiberal democracy is a growth industry," Zakaria wrote in 1997. His prophetic words have an even greater ring of truth at the moment.

In June 2016, the Philippines elected a brash populist named Rodrigo Duterte as its new president. Duterte, who is known as "Duterte Harry"—a pun on "Dirty Harry"—has a history of association with vigilantes and brags about using brute force to control crime and drugs. Once a great heroine of the struggle for democracy, Nobel Laureate Aung San Su Kyi, whose party won the national elections in Myanmar, has turned into a sad apologist for majoritarian politics and genocidal violence against the Rohingya minority. Apart from its failure to prevent the murders of secular bloggers, the government in nearby Bangladesh has increasingly taken an authoritarian path and turned onto its political opponents. Paul Kagame's post-genocide regime in Rwanda, which has been hailed for order and progress by the West, has ruthlessly destroyed freedom of expression and silenced critical voices. As the great philosopher and historian of ideas Isaiah Berlin said, "Freedom for the wolves has often meant death to the sheep."

16   The illiberal tide and the rise of the strongmen exact a terrible human toll. At the end of these academic categories lie individuals and families whose lives are shaped, twisted, and often destroyed. I knew that well from my experience of reporting in India over the years. Through reading and through conversations with friends over time I found strong echoes of the Indian story in Turkey. These are two large democracies, which grew out of the collapse of empires, and which were led by charismatic founding fathers inclined toward varying degrees of European modernity. They are also multi-ethnic and multi-religious societies where religion and secularism are among the dominant faultlines. Both countries have been waging war against ethnic groups on their borders which sought independence or autonomy. India and Turkey are being ruled by strongmen who are business-friendly politicians, men from humble origins, who came of age in traditions of controversial religious politics. Narendra Damodardas Modi and Recep Tayyip Erdoğan also share a love of public speaking, refer to themselves in the third person, and have used hologram technology to speak to multiple audiences across their countries.

I spent a year and a half traveling across India and Turkey. This book isn't merely the story of these powerful politicians but also the story of the men and women they victimized, who showed courage and endured great suffering in their love for true democratic traditions.

India

Part One

The Spell

On a June 2014 afternoon, two weeks after Narendra Modi became Prime Minister of India, I traveled to Ahmedabad, the largest city in the western Indian state of Gujarat. Modi is the son of a tea vendor from a Gujarati village. He left home after high school in the late 1960s to work for the Rashtriya Swayemsevak Sangh, or RSS, an influential Hindu supremacist organization, which seeks to remodel India as a Hindu state.

Modi rose to be the organizational secretary of the group in the mid-eighties. In the fall of 1990, Lal Krishna Advani, then a leading Hindu nationalist politician in the right-wing Bharatiya Janata Party, or BJP, rode across India on a truck designed to look like a chariot from the Hindu epics. The aim of the *yatra*, or political pilgrimage, was to drum up support for building a grand temple to the god Rama in what's believed to be Rama's birthplace, the northern town of Ayodhya—on the

site of a medieval mosque, the Babri Masjid. Two weeks before
the Rama chariot set out on its journey, Modi announced its
itinerary to the press in Ahmedabad, explaining why the grand
temple was crucial to India's national identity. Frenzied crowds
welcomed Advani's chariot in the city—a man stabbed his
arm with a trident and used his gushing blood to put a *tilak*
on Advani's forehead. In villages and towns across India, men
and women gathered to worship the chariot in elaborate Hindu
rituals using incense sticks and sandalwood paste. Militant
young men offered their blood for the cause, calling on Advani
to raze the mosque and build the temple. Indian love for alliteration was mixed with bigotry in the slogans at Advani's
public meetings: *Tel lagao dabur ka, naam mita do Babar ka*—
"Use the hair-oil made by Dabur and erase the name of Babur."
Riots broke out in several states; some 600 people were killed.
On December 6, 1992, tens of thousands of extremist Hindus,
egged on by Hindu nationalist politicians, tore down the Babri
Masjid. This triggered more riots across India that left thousands dead, mostly Muslims.

Modi had earned Advani's confidence when he meticulously
planned a stretch of Advani's *yatra*, as the *yatra* emboldened
Hindu nationalists and the BJP went on to win national elections and form the government in 1998. Advani became Deputy
Prime Minister, while the older, milder Atal Bihari Vajpayee
became Prime Minister. Four years later, Advani appointed
Modi as Chief Minister of Gujarat.

On February 27, 2002, a train carrying dozens of Hindu activists returning from the site of the demolished Babri Masjid

20   in Ayodhya stopped in the town of Godhra. A confrontation between the Hindu activists and Muslim tea vendors ensued. A coach was set on fire—competing political enquiries have yet to settle who lit it—and 59 people were burned alive inside. Their charred bodies were paraded through Ahmedabad.

In the aftermath, armed Hindu mobs fanned through Ahmedabad attacking Muslim homes and businesses. Women were raped and set on fire; children and men were hacked to death. Around 1,000 people, mostly Muslims, were killed. Multiple human rights organizations reported that Modi's government and police officials were complicit in the carnage. Up to 150,000 Muslims took refuge in camps.

Chief Minister Modi not only refused to apologize for his failure to protect his citizens, he called the Muslim camps "child-producing centers." Over the years, Modi has stubbornly refused to show any regret about the carnage on his watch. In 2013, when asked about his lack of remorse, Modi said: "If someone else is driving, and we are sitting in the back seat, and even then if a small puppy comes under the wheel, do we feel pain or not? We do." *Kutte ka baccha* was the Hindi phrase that Modi used, and literally it does mean a puppy. But it is primarily used as a Hindi slur: son of a dog. Modi had chosen his words carefully.

Yet Gujarat would prove to be the perfect state from which Modi could reinvent himself as a man of governance and a pro-business leader.

A wealthy boomtown of about six million people, Ahmedabad witnessed a major expansion during Modi's reign. Real estate prices doubled as corporate parks, luxurious

apartment towers, and shopping malls overran the farming   21
towns on the edges of the city. Modi leveraged the strong economic base of Gujarat, offered sops to large corporations, and
promised to attract lucrative foreign investment.

Although most Indian cities are divided on the basis of religion, in Ahmedabad this division is particularly stark. Muslims,
who constitute about 9 percent of the population, live in slums
on the outskirts, in parts of the walled city, or in Juhapura, a large
ghetto on the city's southwestern edge. Segregation throughout
India increased in the violent aftermath of the demolition of the
Babri Masjid. It became starker, especially in Gujarat, after the
2002 riots. Juhapura, which houses a mixture of working-class
and middle-class Muslims, has no access to basic amenities
such as drinking water, piped gas, and bus service.

The horror of the Gujarat violence—India's first televised
riot—was so overwhelming that in its aftermath, it seemed
impossible that Modi could run for the Indian prime minister's
job. Yet a combination of failures of the ruling Indian Congress
Party, Modi's aggressive success at crafting a new image of himself as an Indian Lee Kwan Yew, and immense support from the
Hindu nationalists and beyond helped him win despite 2002.

When the results of India's 2014 national elections were
declared on May 16, Modi's BJP had won 282 out of 545 seats
in the Lok Sabha ("House of the People"), the lower house of
Parliament. The media called his victory a tsu-NaMo. No politician had won such a popular mandate in India since 1984.

The defining image of the Gujarat riots remains a Reuters photograph of Qutubudin Ansari, a 28-year-old man with thick

A QUESTION OF ORDER

22   wavy hair, standing on the first floor balcony of a house in
Ahmedabad, imploring soldiers from an Indian paramilitary
police force to rescue him. His large, black eyes are filled with
tears, his shirt is bloodstained. The photograph, reproduced in
thousands of newspapers, posters, and pamphlets, became the
emblem of the brutality in Gujarat.

Shortly after arriving in Ahmedabad, I telephoned Ansari to
ask if he would meet with me. I was sure he wouldn't answer; he
has avoided the press since the riots, appearing only at a rally for
the avowedly anti-BJP Communist Party in the southern state
of Kerala during the 2014 election. To my surprise he picked up
after only three rings, speaking in Urdu, the language of northern India. A majority of the city's Muslims, including Ansari's
father, had migrated to Gujarat from the poor northern states of
Uttar Pradesh and Bihar, seeking work in the city's textile mills.
By the mid-1980s, the textile industry had collapsed, after the
government changed its policy to encourage textile manufacturing in smaller, more unorganized sectors, and mill owners
began investing in more lucrative pharmaceutical and chemical
industries. Many of the mill workers became tailors or worked
as cutters in the garment industry, which was owned, predomi-
nantly, by Hindus.

Ansari lives in the working-class area of Sone Ki Chal in
northeastern Ahmedabad, near the shuttered textile mills. We
met by an overpass near his home. In the neighborhood's narrow alleys, I caught glimpses of men bent over sewing machines,
scraps of denim and cotton littering the ground. "Let's go to my
favorite place," Ansari said. "It is very peaceful there." Where
Ansari led me to was a bench on the island that divided the

highway. The Muslims lived in the shantytown on Ansari's side of the highway; the Hindus lived across the divider, in bigger, concrete houses. Ansari pointed to a two-story house with beige tiles and a tiny balcony. "That is where the photograph was taken," he said.

He recalled watching the riots from a hole in a door that opened onto the balcony as mobs looted and burned shops and destroyed homes. Behind him stood his wife, their eldest daughter, and a family friend and his wife. The only exit was a staircase leading to the street. Suddenly Ansari spotted a truck patrolling the street. It belonged to the Rapid Action Force, a federal paramilitary force routinely deployed to control religious riots. He shouted for help. The truck stopped. Ansari ran out onto the balcony and joined his palms in the very Indian gesture of seeking help or forgiveness. Tears rolled down his face as he pleaded for rescue. But the paramilitary men began to pull away. In that moment, Arko Datta, a Reuters photographer who had hitched a ride with the RAF men, snapped a picture of Ansari with his telephoto lens. A minute later, the RAF returned, fired tear gas at the mob, and led Ansari and his family to safety. "Arko and other journalists in the truck forced the RAF to return to save us," Ansari said.

About ten days after the picture was taken, a European journalist found Ansari in a refugee camp and Ansari became famous overnight. For the next few years he struggled with his celebrity. He craved the anonymity and ordinariness of his life before the photograph, which had turned him into the face of the horrors of the Gujarat riots. On the streets Hindu nationalists would recognize him and taunt him: "He is the one who

24   was crying in that picture!" Employers would refuse him work
      as they saw his visible association with the riots as potentially
      troublesome. Liberals and Muslims would flock to him, seeing
      in him a living testament to the failures of Modi and the Hindu
      right. Ansari wanted to be invisible.

      He moved to a town near Mumbai, where his sister lived,
      then to Kolkata, which was ruled by a Communist govern-
      ment critical of the Hindu nationalists. The Communists gave
      him an allowance and a sewing machine and helped him rent a
      shop. But it was difficult to build a clientele in an unknown city.
      After his mother was diagnosed with a heart condition, Ansari
      headed back to Ahmedabad. He resumed his work as a tailor
      and as business picked up, Ansari moved from a rented place to
      his own two-room house, all the while watching Modi growing
      stronger politically and scheming for the prime minister's job.

      Modi had won over a small section of Gujarati Muslims
      through political patronage—a combination of access to state
      resources and a sense of security from future violence and
      prosecution. Displaying just enough visible Muslim support
      was essential to diluting the taint of the 2002 riots. In the fall
      of 2012, Modi began a week-long fast for communal harmony
      known as *Sadhbhavana* ("Goodwill") that would be broadcast on
      Indian television networks. A few days before the show, Modi
      sent several of his Muslim supporters to ask Ansari to come to
      the Sadhbhavana and show his face to the television cameras.
      Ansari threatened to go to the press if he was forced to share the
      stage with Modi. They backed off.

      A year after the Sadhbhavana broadcast, a Muslim who
      worked for Modi's party arrived at Ansari's house. The

government was making a promotional film and they wanted
him to take part along with Amitabh Bachchan, the Bollywood
superstar. Bachchan would say *"Khushboo Hai Gujarat Main"*
("Ah, the scent of Gujarat!") and all Ansari had to do was utter
"Aman Hai Gujarat Main" ("Ah, the peace in Gujarat!") The pay
was good, but Ansari, who makes around 6,000 Indian rupees,
or $100, a month, refused. "My face is my prison but the mem-
ory of the storm too lives in my face," he said.

Voting day in Ahmedabad came in May. Paresh Rawal was
the BJP candidate from Ahmedabad East. Five days later as the
votes were being tallied, Ansari watched the results on his old
television set. Some of his friends joked about Modi's sweep of
the popular vote and the futility of his opposition. Even though
91 percent of India's Muslim voters did not vote for Modi, it
made little difference; consolidation of Hindu votes across
caste divisions made Muslim opposition ineffective.

The most surprising part of the election was the elite embrace
of Modi, even in India's most cosmopolitan city of Mumbai. On
a morning train to Mumbai, a teenager seated next to me had
chosen as the ringtone for his smartphone a chorus of hundreds
of voices chanting: "Modi! Modi! Modi!" The Mumbai elite had
a history of barely voting in Indian elections, relying instead on
influence and connections. But this time they had voted over-
whelmingly for Modi.

I drove for an hour and a half through exacting traffic from
the Mumbai Central railway terminus to Andheri to meet Rahul
Mehra, who is typical of the elite voters Modi has been able
to attract in India's commercial capital. Mehra is 29 years old,

26   educated at Princeton, and worked for a time at a hedge fund
in New York before returning to India in 2008 to run the family hotel businesses. He saw Modi as the great hope for India's
future. After spectacular gains in the 2000s, India's economic
growth sputtered to about 5 percent by the summer of 2013.
Government promises of better electricity, roads, infrastructure,
and jobs for the millions of young Indians graduating college
were fading. "Economically, things were out of control," Mehra
told me. "It was hurting me very bad as a businessman. We were
trying to invest, get land banks, build new hotels, but we couldn't
get permission for our projects." Mehra and his brother turned
from India to Thailand, which gets three times the tourists India
does. They built a new hotel there. "We got loans at 7 percent
interest in Thailand; in India we have to pay 13 percent interest."

Mehra, who lives in a high-end apartment complex in South
Mumbai, had never voted before. But in 2014 members of the
South Mumbai business elite came together to form a lobbying group, India First, to support the Modi's campaign; a friend
persuaded Mehra to join. "We talked about registering voters,
about good governance, and change," Mehra recalled. "We were
impressed by Modi's record in Gujarat. He is very corporate; he
seemed to be someone who is being responsible to his share-
holders. I felt that the Congress government had plundered the
country more than the British did in 150 years. As [Nobel Prize-
winning psychologist] Daniel Kahneman says, a person values a
loss twice as much as he values a gain."

Yet despite the massive corruption under Congress rule,
the Indian elite suffered little when compared with the poor.
Inequality in India is now growing at a faster rate than in other

developing countries like China, Brazil, and Russia. Why, I
wondered, were the rich so angry? "We could have done better,"
Mehra explained. "Like the concentration of wealth at the top,
there was a concentration of anger at the top as well. My neighbor has a steel factory in Karnataka, which has been lying idle
for a few years because he cannot get enough coal for power. It
felt like a lost decade."

India First registered 30,000 voters in South Mumbai, and
set up a call center. When measured against the machinery of
the Modi campaign, the effort wasn't much, but it signified a
new embrace of Hindu nationalists by the globally connected
Indian elite. India First hosted high-profile speakers, including the xenophobic and Islamophobic BJP leader, Subramanian
Swamy, who called for declaring India a Hindu state and for taking away the voting rights of India's non-Hindu citizens.

Behind his desk, Mehra prominently displayed Cornel
West's *Democracy Matters* and Toni Morrison's *Playing in the
Dark*. Mehra had taken a class with West at Princeton. The
works of West and Morrison seemed mere signifiers of an Ivy
League education, markers of cultural capital, objects devoid of
their ideas and politics. I wondered how he reconciled the values
of Morrison and West—unequivocal supporters of civil rights
and diversity—with his enthusiastic support for Narendra
Modi and his party. Mehra was a little uncomfortable with the
history of sectarian violence and the worldview of Modi's BJP
and its parent group, the RSS. "Their history is disturbing but
the Congress too has skeletons in its cupboard," he said. He was
referring to the 1984 massacre of 3,000 Sikhs in New Delhi after
the assassination of Prime Minister Indira Gandhi by her Sikh

28　　bodyguards. Three decades later, the perpetrators from the officially secular Congress Party have yet to be convicted. Modi's
supporters often spoke of the 2002 Gujarat riots and the 1984
carnage as if the two pogroms canceled each other out. "But
time heals," Mehra continued. "What we need right now is an
economic agenda."

Few places symbolize the economic promise of India as much
as Hyderabad, the information technology capital of India.
Hyderabad was traditionally a slow-paced city proud of its traditions of courtesy and grace. Its skyline was dominated by the
palaces, tombs, and mosques built by the Nizams, Hyderabad's
pre-independence Muslim rulers. The information technology
district is built on the periphery, on farmland that was appro-
priated after India opened up its state-controlled economy in
the early 1990s. Cyber Towers, a circular glass and steel office
complex built in 1998, marks the beginning of what is known as
HITEC City or Cyberabad.

Before Microsoft, Infosys, Oracle, and Toshiba, among others, built their own corporate parks, they worked out of Cyber
Towers. Google arrived in 2004 and Facebook followed in 2010.
Chandra Babu Naidu, then Chief Minister of Andhra Pradesh,
earned the moniker "Laptop Chief Minister"; Naidu was credited
for putting his weight behind the transformation of Hyderabad
into an information technology powerhouse between 1999 and
2004. In the past decade and half, several thousand cyber towers
have sprung up. (In 2013, Telangana split from Andhra Pradesh
and became its own state, with Hyderabad as the new capital.) IT
exports from Hyderabad during 2013–14 were about $10 billion;

the city provided employment to as many as 450,000 people.

I'd stopped in Hyderbad to meet V. Rohit Kashyap, an engineer who ran the social media campaign for Modi and his party in undivided Andhra Pradesh, which sent 42 lawmakers to Parliament. The Modi campaign was fought in village processions, but also on social media. Some of the most strident voices of the Hindu right working in support of Modi came from the world of engineering and information technology.

Kashyap works at Back Office Associates, a data firm which attracted investments from Goldman Sachs. We met at the Heart Cup, a café and bar in Cyberabad popular with IT professionals. A small, somber man who wore the caste mark of a Brahmin on his forehead, 27-year-old Kashyap comes from a family affiliated with the RSS for three generations. Members of the RSS attend early morning assemblies at *shakhas*, or local chapters, where they receive ideological indoctrination and paramilitary training. But Kashyap was a frail boy; his engineer father suspected he was too weak to bear the physical rigors and the mental pressures of a political life in the RSS. "They kept me away from it," Kashyap said. His voice was taut with anger at that old slight, the haunting parental assumption of his puniness.

In 2005, Kashyap moved to Guntur, a town 160 miles south of Hyderabad, to study mechanical engineering at a university there. He was 18. He was struck by the intensity of the caste tensions in his college. "Even in the classroom, students sat according to their caste," he recalled. One day he made a snide remark about Balakrishna, a popular actor and the son of legendary lower-caste actor-politician N. T. Rama Rao, who broke the hegemony of Brahmins and other upper-castes in Andhra

30   Pradesh in the early eighties by forming his own political party
       and ruling the state for almost two decades. His lower-caste
       classmates interpreted the remark as stemming from his upper-
       caste, Brahmin prejudice. "I was beaten up," Kashyap recalled.
       A Marxist professor consoled and supported him. Under that
       professor's influence, Kashyap began to reevaluate his feelings
       about caste prescriptions and Hinduism's role in creating them.
       It marked the beginning of a shift in his politics, he says, toward
       the extreme left.

       On a visit home, his father sensed his son was slipping
       out of the fold. He gave Kashyap a CD of the lectures of Swami
       Vivekananda, a Hindu revivalist from the nineteenth century,
       whose speeches about universal truths being behind all faiths
       were admired by Leo Tolstoy and Aldous Huxley. Vivekananda
       expressed qualified critiques of the caste system, and his work
       was appropriated by post-colonial Hindu nationalists for
       propagating a modernist, muscular Hinduism. I remembered
       the BJP's student wing would paste posters of Vivekananda
       on the walls of Delhi University in the late nineties: a robust,
       young man with large eyes in a turban, his muscular arms folded
       across his chest. His words: Strength is life; weakness is death.
       Kashyap's readings of Vivekananda increased his zeal. "I real-
       ized that caste discrimination is not a problem specific to India
       because America and Europe also have this problem," Kashyap
       said. "They call it racism. The argument that it is only Hinduism
       that oppresses lower castes simply does not hold."

       After graduating in 2008, Kashyap traveled with his father
       to their ancestral home in Kurnool village. Certain of his ideo-
       logical moorings, of the Hindu nationalist path, Kashyap asked

his father to initiate him into the RSS by taking him to a *shakha*.
One day in 2009, Kashyap heard a speech by Mohan Bhagwat,
the supreme leader of the RSS. "He said that for a civilization and nation, three things are needed: Identity, Credibility,
Character," Kashyap recalled. "It really touched my heart."

But as he said so, his face hardened, and he began to explain
why Hindus needed to take pride in their heritage. "We feel
inferior to *gora chamda* (white skin). We think all the Nobel lau-
reates come from the West and we are good for nothing. Very
few people know that if Nobel prizes were awarded on the past
achievements, be it medicine, be it physics, be it chemistry,
Indians would have won hands down." He spoke about how the
Vedas, the ancient Hindu texts, had calculated the speed of light
with utmost precision, how Indians knew the antiseptic value
of turmeric for centuries (women who did household work
barefoot used turmeric to protect their feet), how Susrutha, a
Brahmin, performed the first surgery in history. "You know, ants
bite!" Kashyap said. "He used ants to cut a patient's skin and
stitch. Google him."

A few months after our meeting, Modi echoed Kashyap's
sentiments about the scientific feats of ancient Indians while
speaking at the inaugural ceremony of a hospital in Mumbai.
"We worship Lord Ganesha," Modi told his audience, referring
to the elephant-headed Hindu god Ganesha. "There must have
been some plastic surgeon at that time who got an elephant's
head on the body of a human being and began the practice of
plastic surgery."

Kashyap had the manner of a much older man. His sense
of mission and the intensity of his large brown eyes made him

32   an outlier among the bantering, flirtatious men and women patronizing the café. He was aghast at what India remembered of its past. "A student of history today will tell you he read about Robert Clive, Shahjahan and Aurangzeb," he said, referring to a British adventurer and two Mughal emperors. "Stop glorifying people who invaded and conquered our country. Why do we still espouse Mughal culture? Why do we have a street in New Delhi still named after Aurangzeb?" (Aurangzeb Road was renamed in 2015 to A. P. J. Abdul Kalam Road, after the Muslim scientist who was tactically appointed by the BJP government in 2002 as President of India, and his acceptance of the ceremonial presidential position helped Hindu nationalists ease the taint of the Gujarat carnage.) These were the "historical wrongs" he sought to correct by going into politics. His Twitter bio prominently mentioned the goal of India as *Hindu Rashtra*, a Hindu nation. "It requires a transformation, the way we teach history, the way we inculcate a sense of pride in our past and history," he told me. In Narendra Modi, he saw someone who thought like he did. "I could connect every time he spoke. He always makes his pride in India, in our history and our civilization, very clear. I was able to connect."

Kashyap formally joined the information technology cell of the BJP in Andhra Pradesh in 2010, and four years later he was leading the party's social media campaign in the region. His focus was on getting the urban youth to vote for Modi. "They might not read the morning papers, but the urban youth do start their day with Facebook and Twitter," he explained. "So we went where they were." He trawled the comments pages of popular television network websites and various Facebook

groups. He identified users whose comments echoed his own
ideology. "If he was from our area, I would send him a friend
request and request a private phone conversation," Kashyap
explained. He would invite the potential convert for dinner at
a restaurant or at his house. Kashyap's team built a network
of 2,000 social media warriors for Modi and his party. "I per-
sonally met around five hundred people." Most of the people
Kashyap enlisted were engineers and information technology
professionals. "We are used to corporate culture where merit is
appreciated. Our CEO's son does not become the CEO. When
the techies see the Congress Party and its dynastic practices,
they cannot relate to it."

One of the biggest challenges on Modi's road to prime minis-
tership remained the traditional opposition of the lower and
middle castes to his party, especially in the northern Indian
states of Bihar and Uttar Pradesh. The two states elect 120 lawmakers to the Lok Sabha, more than a fifth of all members.

In Bihar, Modi was challenging the coalition of two veteran politicians: Laloo Prasad Yadav, a former Chief Minister of
the state, who empowered the lower caste and prevented sectarian violence but had also faced serious graft charges during
his term, and Nitish Kumar, who defeated Yadav to take over as
Chief Minister in 2005. Kumar was praised for strengthening
infrastructure and improving security and safety in Bihar, and
he ruled in a coalition with the BJP until he broke with them
in 2013, when Modi was chosen as the candidate for prime
minister. Kumar, a believer in pluralism, found Modi's majoritarianism unacceptable. "I cannot work with anyone who poses

34   a challenge to that idea, I will fight such a person, I will fight
      such an idea," he told his biographer.

      Jadhua is a small village 15 miles north of Patna, the capital
      of Bihar. The traffic moved slowly, becoming nearly impassable
      once I reached a massive bridge over the River Ganges that linked
      Patna and the northern parts of the state. Jadhua's proximity to
      Patna and Kumar's infrastructure projects have brought rela-
      tive prosperity to the village—expansive multi-story houses sit
      beside tiny, cramped huts; young men on motorcycles race past
      buffaloes and cows grazing lazily in the alleys.

      There I met Dinesh Prasad, a 46-year-old guard with the
      Indian railways, who lives in a three-room brick house at the edge
      of the village. As we sat on red plastic chairs, Prasad talked about
      the history of bitter caste divisions in Bihar. "Laloo Yadav is my
      god," Prasad told me. "Because of him we lived without the fear
      of upper castes, because of him we got jobs in government." He
      planned to vote for Yadav in state elections in the winter, but in
      2014 it didn't matter that he and his lower- and middle-caste
      neighbors had always supported Yadav and the Congress Party,
      who now were staunchly opposed to the BJP; he was won over
      by Modi's aggressive, authoritarian personality. Modi had fielded
      a blistering campaign in the state that focused on his economic
      record in Gujarat, middle-caste origins, polarizing Hindu nation-
      alistic rhetoric, and embodiment of a muscular strongman.

      "Manmohan Singh is meek, he could barely speak," Prasad
      said. "If the head of your house is so weak, then the neighbors
      will mess with you. Pakistan's army came and cut the heads of
      our soldiers and Manmohan Singh did nothing. China threatens
      us on our borders and they do nothing. We needed a strong man,

a powerful man to lead India. If Pakistan cuts heads of two of our soldiers, Modi will chop off twenty Pakistani heads."

Modi carried the impoverished, semi-feudal Bihar by an unexpectedly wide margin, winning over aspiring youths as well as members of the lower and middle castes, like Prasad—the traditional voters for Kumar and Yadav.

At a campaign rally in late April, Giriraj Singh, a leader of the BJP from Bihar, who is devoted to Modi and Hindu nationalist politics, declared that there will be no place for Modi's critics in India. "Those who intend to stop Narendra Modi are looking at Pakistan. In the coming days, there won't be any place for them in India, or in Jharkhand, but Pakistan." Modi appointed Singh as the junior minister for enterprise in his government.

One early July 2014 morning, I arrived in Varanasi, the holiest Hindu city, in Uttar Pradesh. As street lamps flickered in the blue dawn, I watched crowds of Hindu pilgrims walk briskly through narrow, serpentine alleys, past crumbling houses to the Ganges riverfront. From wooden poles by the riverbank fluttered the saffron flags of the BJP. "Mother Ganges has called me," Modi declared during a campaign stop in late April. As he spoke, Amit Shah, a former minister in Gujarat and Modi's closest aide, stood on his right. Shah had been running the Modi campaign in Uttar Pradesh. A burly, balding man in his early fifties, Shah faces charges for the murder of three people the police suspect of plotting to assassinate Modi as revenge for the 2002 anti-Muslim violence. Shah, who insists the murder charges are politically motivated, also has the reputation of being a brilliant and ruthless political strategist.

I fully understood Shah's shrewd political acumen only after meeting one of his workers, Rajneesh Singh, inside a gaudy shopping mall and office complex a few miles from the Varanasi riverfront. Singh, an athletic man in his mid-thirties from an upper-caste landlord family from a village near Varanasi, wore aviator shades and body-hugging shirts popularized by Bollywood star Salman Khan. Singh ran a small construction company in partnership with a BJP legislator he met at an RSS training camp. Like Modi in his youth, Singh worked as a propagandist and outreach worker for the RSS. Singh had campaigned for the BJP in many elections; but after Shah took over Modi's campaign in Utter Pradesh, the organization gained new energy. As Singh saw it, "Amit Shah came with a new plan that he had tested in Gujarat." Singh recalled excitedly how he implemented one of Shah's ideas for ensuring maximum polling for a BJP candidate.

The sheer numbers of voters in Indian elections can be daunting for anyone trying to make sure supporters get to the polls. In the 2014 election, 814 million Indians voted in 930,000 polling stations. On average, each polling station caters to around 900 voters, who are listed in a sheaf of paper about 15 pages thick. Shah's organizational insight was to create a new position of "page supervisor," a volunteer responsible for persuading the 60-odd voters on a single page of the list to vote for the BJP. India had never witnessed such meticulous planning to get out the vote. "It amounts to being responsible for ten families in your neighborhood," Singh explained. "Every page supervisor looked after his own family and other families who live next door, people he knows. He ensured that they came out on the day of voting, that they knew lotus was the electoral symbol for the BJP and Modi." I asked Singh if I could meet a page supervisor. He pointed toward the man who had served us tea.

A few hundred miles from Varanasi, the western region of Uttar Pradesh and the abutting state of Haryana form a belt of prosperous middle-caste, land-owning Hindu Jats. The area remains culturally conservative and is infamous for honor killings and female feticide. While Modi spoke of development and governance throughout his campaign, it was in Western Uttar Pradesh that his party's strategy of religious polarization between Hindus and Muslims, and the exploitation of sectarian tensions to bring various caste groups under the saffron banner of the BJP, became visible.

Muzaffarnagar and Shamli districts in Western Uttar Pradesh, about 80 miles north of New Delhi, are dominated by miles of sugarcane fields, which form the core of the area's economy. I met Gul Bahar, a 20-year-old college student from Lisarh, a relatively prosperous village of 8,000 people around 35 miles from Muzaffarnagar town, which is the center of the eponymous district. Muslims once made up about a third of its population. But in late August 2013, intense sectarian violence broke out in several area villages. The troubles began after two Hindu Jats killed a Muslim youth who allegedly harassed the sister of one of the men. They were in turn killed by a group of Muslims who were arrested for the murder, but rumors spread that they were released without charge.

Hindu Jats already saw the ruling socialist Samajwadi Party as partial to Muslims; Jats in the district traditionally voted

38   for a regional party allied with the Congress Party. The BJP saw an opening. They held rallies and made incendiary speeches, arousing passions further.

About two weeks later, Hindu Jats held a *panchayat*, an assembly of villagers, to "save the honor of daughters and daughters-in-law." Thousands attended. In videos of the meeting, young Jat men carrying scythes, rods, and swords shouted anti-Muslim slurs. Politicians from the BJP led the gathering, making provocative speeches. Hukum Singh, a BJP leader, roared: "The purpose of this *panchayat* is Hindu unity." On their way to the assembly, Hindus stabbed two Muslims; on their way back, Muslims retaliated and killed thirteen Hindus, according to police officials. As word of the attacks spread, mobs of Hindu Jats began attacking Muslim homes in surrounding villages.

Bahar was home with his extended family when he heard the terrifying roar outside his house. A crowd armed with knives, scythes, country-made pistols, and swords flooded his street. Some carried jerry cans filled with gasoline. "They began setting our homes on fire," Bahar recalled. "They attacked whomever they saw." Bahar and his family escaped through the sugarcane fields surrounding their village and walked through the night. His family took shelter in the largely Muslim village of Kandhla. His grandfather, Mohammad Sukkan, a retired farmer in his early seventies, refused to leave.

As Bahar and his family settled into a refugee camp, they waited for news of Sukkan. "Thirteen people from our village were killed," Bahar told me. "Only two bodies were found." Eventually, police discovered Sukkan's body in a canal, fifteen miles from Lisarh. Bahar showed me the photograph of his slain grandfather that the police gave the family. The body was covered in a white sheet; the head, severed from the neck by a sharp object, lay by the torso.

More than 40,000 people, mostly Muslims, were displaced from their homes. Sixty-two people were killed. After a few weeks, Bahar and a few others visited Lisarh. "They had burnt our houses," he recalled. "Our stuff lay scattered in the alleys. I couldn't bear to look at it." In the spring, they moved with a few other families to a patch of agricultural land in Kandhla, a mile from their refugee camp. A few months later, government assistance provided to families victimized by the violence allowed them to buy a patch of land and rebuild a house of bare bricks. "Our village is eight kilometers from here but we can't return home," he said.

The violence drew a stark boundary through the region. Amit Shah, the Modi strategist, nominated several BJP politicians facing charges for inciting violence for the national elections. On the campaign trail, Shah described the polls as "an election for honor, for seeking revenge for the insult, and for teaching a lesson to those who committed injustice."

At another public meeting in Muzaffarnagar, Shah returned to a subject Modi had spoken of earlier: that the Congress Party promoted slaughterhouses and the export of meat through tax breaks—a process he described as a Pink Revolution, referencing a speech Modi had given in Bihar lamenting the spread of large abattoirs across India. "When animals are killed, the color of their flesh is pink," Modi said. "If you want to rear cows, the Congress government won't give you any subsidy, but it offers subsidies to those who slaughter cows, to those who slaughter

40   animals." Although India's meat exporters and traders include
      Hindus and Christians, many of those associated with the
      industry are Muslim. "Beggars have turned millionaires by
      running butcher houses," Shah said, according to a report in
      Scroll. India's national election commission censured Shah for
      his derogatory remarks and banned him from campaigning for
      a while. But after the BJP won 71 of 80 seats in Uttar Pradesh,
      Modi, deploying a cricket metaphor, described Shah as "the
      man of the match."

      The violence in Muzaffarnagar and the incendiary rhetoric
      during the campaign polarized the state on religious lines, unit-
      ing Hindu voters across the barriers of caste to vote for Modi
      and the BJP. One afternoon, as I drove through the crowded
      bazaars of Muzaffarnagar, posters of the Hollywood action
      movie *Expendables* 3 competed for attention with the faces of
      Hindu and Muslim politicians. A potholed road led off the town
      square to Khaderwala, a lower middle class neighborhood a few
      miles away, where many of Muzaffarnagar's Dalits live.

      Ram Kumar is among the wave of Dalit voters who helped
      Modi and Shah win the "match." The 31-year-old tailor lives
      with his family in a three-room house on a narrow street in
      Khaderwala. Kumar and his neighbors always voted for the
      Bahujan Samaj Party, led by Kumari Mayawati, who became the
      first Dalit Chief Minister of Uttar Pradesh in 1995. Mayawati,
      who was 39 and unmarried when first elected Chief Minister in
      1995, embodied a sense of dignity and power for India's lowest
      castes, who suffered centuries of oppression. People referred to
      her as Behenji, an honorific for elder sister. A shrewd political
      operator, Mayawati was elected to lead India's most populous

state four times. But in the recent campaign dominated by Modi, she chose mostly non-Dalit candidates, hoping to reach out to non-Dalit voters. "Behenji forgot us, neglected us, and assumed that we will always vote for her," Kumar said.

His turn from Dalit activism to Hindu nationalism was also prompted by the religious violence and tensions in Muzaffarnagar. After the riots, Muzaffarnagar was under military curfew for almost two weeks. Kumar walked me to the main street, which I had taken to reach his neighborhood. He pointed to an utility pole a few blocks away. "The Muslims live beyond that," he said. He turned around and pointed toward a stretch of bigger houses. "There you have Jats, Brahmins, and other upper castes." The Dalits lived in the middle. In the riots, Kumar said, the Dalits and upper-caste Hindus fell on one side of an unmarked boundary and the Muslims on the other side. "Nobody crossed from the Hindu area into the Muslim area for about a month," he told me. The Dalits found little support from Mayawati during that volatile season. "It was the people from the BJP who stood by us here." The Indian constitution reserves 17 of the 80 seats of the Lok Sabha for the Dalits; Modi's candidates won them all.

The highway from Lucknow to Ayodhya, where Lal Krishna Advani wanted to build a grand Rama temple, cuts through empty fields and sparsely populated villages. On the banks of the ancient Sarayu River flanking the town, a group of old Brahmins sought refuge from the heat under a tree and played cards. Pilgrims ran down flights of stairs and bathed with their clothes on. The old temples—their domes a combination of

42   Hindu and Muslim influences—looked run down, their façades peeling, in need of a coat of paint. It was a rather quaint scene for a place that had come to symbolize the strivings of Hindu nationalist politics, in whose name Advani furiously tore apart the country's civic life and irrevocably broke the consensus of Nehruvian secularism as the religion of India.

For a few hours every day, pilgrims are allowed to visit and pray at the makeshift temple that marks Rama's birthplace on the foundation of the mosque Advani worked to demolish. Armed police and paramilitary troops stood guard along the road to the site, which is officially known as Babri Mosque-Ram Birthplace. A row of shops sold everything from Hindu scriptures, copies of *Arthashastra*, plastic idols of Hindu gods, and DVDs showing the demolition of the mosque.

After being frisked at several checkpoints, I passed through a metal detector and entered a tunnel, just a few feet wide, covered by an aluminum wire mesh. I noticed sandbags and more soldiers with machine guns in the grassy ground beyond. About half a mile into the tunnel, in an opening in the wire mesh, two Hindu priests collected offerings behind a counter. Behind the priests, on a small patch of flat earth, was the makeshift temple built after the demolition of the Babri Masjid. I recognized a few idols of Rama and his wife Sita. A mound of exposed earth lay around it. I failed to see even a fragment of an arch, a section of the broken dome. The erasure of the mosque was complete. I left with a feeling that it was not the construction of the temple but the erasure of the mosque that seemed to have moved the Hindu nationalists.

As I walked back through the wire mesh tunnel, I got a call
from Sandeep Trivedi, a young Brahmin from Faizabad, a few
miles from Ayodhya. Trivedi had served as a wireless operator
with a paramilitary force in my hometown in Indian-controlled
Kashmir. After a few years, he left the force and found work as
a civilian in New Delhi. We met in one of the few restaurants in
Faizabad; the restaurant had bright red chairs and a large aquar-
ium. Trivedi talked about Ayodhya, Faizabad, and the scores
of villages around the conjoined towns. "Two criminal gangs
attacked each other in the courtroom yesterday," he said. "We
have no working streetlights." He lamented the world's focus on
Ayodhya's religious and political histories and the utter neglect
of civic amenities. "We don't even have a sewage system that
works."

What most frustrated Trivedi was the region's anemic
healthcare system. At a certain point in the election campaign,
a young woman from his wife's family, who was expecting her
first child, was moved to a hospital in Faizabad. The local doctors didn't have the equipment for the medical tests she needed.
The family was told that a hospital in Lucknow, 78 miles away,
could help her, so they drove her there. "She lost her child on
the way," he told me. As the new globalized economy evaded
small provincial towns, their decay accelerated, and the middle
class continued to flee to glossy urban centers. "Anyone who
can afford to buy or rent an apartment in Lucknow or New Delhi
leaves Ayodhya and Faizabad," Trivedi said. He hoped a new government might do better, and voted for Modi.

Freedom for the Wolf

The Indian equivalent of the State of the Union address is the Prime Minister's speech on August 15, Independence Day, from the splendid Red Fort in Delhi. In his first speech from the Red Fort, Modi spoke eloquently and forcefully to convey a surprisingly inclusive vision of India. He promised to work for "the welfare of mother India, and also for the welfare of the poor, oppressed, Dalits, the exploited and the backward people of our country." He spoke of better governance and accountability to realize the dreams of millions of Indians and sought support for greater common good. He agonized about increased violence against women in India.

Modi then spoke about a subject few expected him to bring up: religious strife and violence in India. "Brothers and sisters, for one reason or the other, we have had communal [sectarian] tensions for ages. This led to the division of the country,"

Modi said. The reference was to the Partition of British-ruled   45
India into the nation states of India and Pakistan in August
1947, which was accompanied by genocidal violence between
Hindus, Sikhs, and Muslims, killing around two million and
displacing about 10 million people. "Even after Independence,
we have had to face the poison of casteism and communalism.
How long will these evils continue?" Modi asked. He went
on to describe prejudice and violence stemming from caste-
based, region-based, and religion-based politics as a major
obstacle for India's progress. "Let us resolve for once in our
hearts, let us put a moratorium on all such activities for ten
years; we shall march ahead to a society which will be free from
all such tensions. And you will see how much strength we get
from peace, unity, goodwill, and brotherhood. Try it out once!
Leave the path of old sins!"

I replayed that section of the video of his speech several times. Modi is a powerful orator; the speech from the Red
Fort was among his best. Was Modi setting aside his controversial, sectarian past and reinventing himself as a liberal,
all-embracing Prime Minister of India?

Two days before Modi spoke at the Red Fort, there was a
debate in Parliament on a law regarding sectarian violence. Yogi
Adityanath, a member of Parliament and the leader of the BJP in
Uttar Pradesh, was chosen as the opening speaker of the party.
He was confident and calm as he began, and he seemed con-
scious of his enormous audience: the proceedings were being
televised nationally. Adityanath, a robust 42-year-old man
who shaves his head and wears the regulation saffron robes of a
Hindu priest, is also the head of a powerful Hindu seminary and

46   temple in the city of Gorakhpur. He has become one of the most popular faces of Hindu supremacist rhetoric.

Adityanath forcefully told Parliament that the Hindu majority of India had been victimized, that the country's secular and left parties had conspired against the Hindu society and showered benefits and privileges on minority groups in the name of secularism. "The Hindu is the symbol of India's nationalism," Adityanath roared. "Those who try to defame Hindutva will have to pay the price." Lawmakers from the BJP thumped their desks, egging him on. Adityanath described conspiracies against Hinduism and urged Indians to retaliate.

Modi's inclusive Red Fort speech turned out to be an excellent piece of theater aimed at national and global headlines. Days after Adityanath and Modi spoke, the BJP chose Adityanath to run an electoral campaign in Uttar Pradesh. Several seats in the state legislature had fallen vacant for various reasons and new legislators would be elected in a new poll for those seats—an exercise known as "by-polls." Adityanath signaled his electoral campaign would follow the path of blatant sectarian politics. "The issue of love jihad would certainly be an issue in this by-poll," he said.

The phrase "love jihad" had been added to the lexicon of hate a few years earlier. Hindu nationalists accused young Indian Muslim men of seducing Hindu women and converting them to Islam, labeling it a new kind of jihadist activity. Hindu Jagruti ("Awareness"), a prominent Hindu nationalist website, claimed that Muslim men were being funded by Islamists in Saudi Arabia to perform love jihad.

Initially such declarations evoked ridicule, but the gravity of the fear-mongering campaign and the danger it posed

to the fraught civic relations in India sank in when the BJP and
the RSS put their weight behind the conspiracy theory and
sought to use it to garner potential Hindu voters. *Panchjanya*,
the Hindi language house journal of the RSS, which wields
enormous influence on the cadre and leadership of the Hindu
nationalist family, published a cover story on love jihad. Its
cover image was striking: a Muslim man in a red and white *kef-
fiyeh*, sporting a goatee, wearing black wayfarers with red hearts
photoshopped on the lenses. In the article, Hitesh Shankar, the
editor of *Panchjanya*, referenced the work of British primatologist Jane Goodall, who "observed that [chimpanzees] don't let
other species enter the part of the forest they occupy but the
male chimpanzees loiter on the borders of their territory to
seduce females from other groups. They try to seduce maximum number of females and procreate generously to increase
the numerical strength of their group."

"The notion of 'love jihad' is a classic example of a majoritarian party trying to tap into a sense of passive-aggressive
injury," argued Mukul Kesavan, a leading liberal essayist. "In
the Indian context this consists of riffing on several related
themes: we-are-peaceful-but-they-are-predatory, we-don't-
convert-but-they-steal-our-daughters, if-this-goes-on-we'll-
be-a-minority-soon." Modi chose to stay silent, not uttering a
word of rebuke, which came across as tacit approval.

The lexicon of majoritarian politics was expanding as the
months went by. Niranjan Jyoti, a minister in the Modi government, combined bigotry with alliteration. "You have to chose
whether Ramzaade will form the government or the Haramzaade
will," Jyoti said during a campaign speech, smiling. Ramzaade

48   means the progeny of the Hindu god Rama; Haramzaade means bastards. Jyoti offered voters the simple choice of being for the Hindu nationalists or against them.

A few days later, activists affiliated with the RSS introduced a new campaign: Ghar Wapsi, Hindi for homecoming. The aim was to "bring home" or reconvert the Hindus who had supposedly previously "left for" Christianity or Islam.

A photograph from the slum of Ved Nagar, a few miles from the Taj Mahal, became the emblem of Ghar Wapsi. In the photograph, a plump Hindu priest is adding a handful of scripturally designated ingredients—bits of sandalwood, some flower petals—to a ritualistic fire burning between a square of bricks. A gaunt young man with a moustache is imitating the priest, his hand extended toward the fire. The young man holds the saffron flag of Hinduism in his left hand and wears a Muslim skullcap. A small group of Muslim men in skullcaps huddle around the fire; some women squat behind them. Several children and young boys stand behind the men. The faces of the children are somber and curious. The men with skullcaps have the same expression of strain and curiosity on their faces. A caption below the photograph reads: *Slum dwellers participating in a Ghar Wapsi ceremony.*

The "slum dwellers" turned out to be among the poorest, most vulnerable Muslims of the area—immigrants from Bangladesh who managed to make a living by collecting and manually recycling garbage and trash and ferrying local passengers on the cycle rickshaws they pedaled throughout punishing winters and summers. In return for converting, activists from a group affiliated with the RSS offered them legal documentation that would help them get subsidized food and health insurance,

among other federal benefits for India's poorest. The incident
grabbed national attention. The local government arrested the
Hindu nationalist leader who orchestrated the conversion ceremony, and the "converts" returned to being Muslim and poor in
a few weeks.

After intense criticism from opposition parties, Modi
broke his silence, spoke about respect for all religions, and
asked his party leader not to cross that particular line. Modi's
words had some effect, but prominent Hindu nationalist leaders continued speaking in favor of converting Christians and
Muslims. Six months later, the World Hindu Council, one of
the biggest affiliates of the RSS and the BJP, produced its annual
report on the Ghar Wapsi campaign. The group claimed that in
one year it prevented around 48,000 Hindus from converting
and "brought back" more than 30,000 people to Hinduism. "All
minorities in India have converted from Hinduism," Champat
Rai, General Secretary of the World Hindu Council declared in
an interview. "They should accept their original faith."

The winter of religious conversions gave way to a spring of dietary
policing. The stage of political drama moved to Mumbai, the
capital of the western Indian state of Maharashtra. Modi's BJP
ran the state government in coalition with Shiv Sena, a militant
right-wing party, which combines Hindu nationalism with ethnic
chauvinism. When they had formed their first coalition government in the mid-1990s, they managed a linguistic Ghar Wapsi for
the capital city and changed its name from Bombay to Mumbai.

In 1995, the first year of its rule in Bombay, BJP-Shiv Sena
lawmakers amended the Maharashtra Animal Preservation Act

50   to expand a ban on cow slaughter to include the killing of bulls and bullocks too. The bill languished in India's bureaucratic and political labyrinths for about two decades. In March 2015, the President of India, Pranab Mukherjee, took it up and gave his nod to turn the amended bill into law.

Slaughter of a cow, a bull, or a bullock became a crime in one of the richest and biggest states of India. Selling or possessing beef became a criminal offense with a five-year prison term. India is the largest exporter of beef in the world and its fifth biggest consumer. Beef is considered the poor man's protein and is consumed by Dalits and Muslims on the lower end of the economic ladder—along with a section of the upper-middle classes and the elite, who enjoy a steak or a burger in high-end restaurants. The politics over cows (and bulls) served the majoritarian project, emphasizing the difference between the believers and the "beef-eating other." Modi once told a reporter from *Outlook* magazine, "People who eat meat have a different temperament." In classic dog-whistle politics, it added to the idea of the violent other, those who kill and eat holy animals.

Mohammad Ali Road is a noisy, oppressively crowded thoroughfare in southern Mumbai. It is a mostly Muslim area choked with a mixture of tiny apartments and equally cramped, hectic business establishments. It is the chaos and energy of Mumbai on speed. In an alley branching off the main street, I met Karim Ansari, a 46-year-old butcher who had migrated as a boy from a village in northern India to Mumbai to make his fortune, and still calls the city Bombay. "I worked as an errand boy at a meat shop for years. I slept on the sidewalk," Ansari, who had betel-nut-stained teeth and an easy smile, recalled.

"Bombay makes you work and then Bombay provides. I own my shop now, I own my house." Ansari not only sold meat from his store off Mohammad Ali Road, he also supplied small shop owners. Most of his customers were from the lower-middle class and preferred beef. "I am selling buffalo meat but the ban has cut my business by half," he told me. "Families which came to buy meat twice a week, now show up twice a month. They can't afford goat or chicken."

Ansari knew the world of beef production and sale in India. He took pride in being able to look at a bull or a buffalo in a cattle market and guess its weight correctly. A friend who lived nearby had led me to his shop. Ansari turned to him and said, "You are around 75 kilos." But he spoke angrily about the BJP trying to use beef to create antipathy against Muslims, who dominate the beef trade in the state. "They are always dividing people into Hindu and Muslim for votes," he said. "I have been buying animals for twenty years from cattle markets everywhere. Who do I buy the animals from? I buy my animals from Hindu businessmen. Who processes the animal hides? It is the lower-caste Hindus who do that."

The specter of the holy cow began to haunt India after Modi and his colleagues politicized the issue. News reports began mentioning the term "cow vigilantes." Stories of cattle traders being beaten up began to appear. Vengeance in the name of the mythical sanctity of an animal was bubbling up like molten rock. In early August 2015, three Muslim men, reportedly cattle smugglers, were beaten to death by a mob in a village on the periphery of Delhi. The killings went largely unnoticed. "The precise alchemy that makes one particular death politically totemic while others go unmourned beyond their families and

52   communities is not quite clear," wrote *Guardian* columnist Gary
      Younge. But the lynching of Mohammad Akhlaq in September
      2015 on the suspicion of him eating beef became the politically
      totemic death that could not go unmourned.

      I drove on a motorway across the toxic, dying river Yamuna,
      crossing the city to Bishara, the village where Akhlaq had died.
      The road followed the rapacious expansion of the metropolis
      creeping up on the rural periphery—steel, glass, and concrete
      replacing the wheat and rice stalks rising from the red earth.
      Several miles before Dadri, the scrappy town near Bishara,
      the highway gave way to a dusty and potholed road. Billboards
      changed from displays of luxury cars to announcements of vil-
      lage wrestling matches. Bishara is a cluster of about a hundred
      homes circled by fields stretching for miles beyond the vil-
      lage. Its brick and cement homes—with a preference for pink
      and yellow façades—suggested a degree of prosperity. Akhlaq
      and his brother Jaan Mohammad lived in adjoining two-story
      houses on a mostly Hindu street. About a mile away, at the other
      end of the village, some Muslim families of farmhands, con-
      struction workers, and carpenters lived beside their landowning
      Hindu neighbors. Some landowning Hindus had helped build
      the small, storefront-style village mosque.

      Akhlaq worked as the village ironsmith for most of his life.
      Easy banter with village folk at his shop flowed between hard
      blows bending their shovels, sickles, cleavers, or cane knives
      to shape. He was prone to scolding truant village boys. He had
      ensured that his two sons and daughter did not neglect their
      education—their sole way out of Bishara. His oldest son, Sartaj,
      had graduated from college and joined the Indian Air Force as

a technician. Danish, Sartaj's younger brother, had graduated
with a degree in economics and was studying for the elite Indian
Civil Service examination. Shahida, their sister, was in the village high school. "He would lecture everyone about school and
college, scold them about wasting time," Sartaj recalled. "But
the mood changed after the Muzaffarnagar riots." The sectarian
violence, a few hours away, emphasized his religious identity.
The hectoring village ironsmith was now seen as the hectoring
Muslim. "He stopped lecturing."

Sartaj was posted at an Air Force base in the southern city
of Chennai, 1,400 miles from Bishara. On a visit home a year
earlier, he saw how the growing antipathy had silenced his
father. One evening he was walking across the village to visit
the mosque. A group of Hindu boys were hanging out by a street
corner. A short, athletic man, Sartaj carried himself with the
alert, brisk gait of a soldier. "You want to buckle the road," one of
the boys shouted. "Watch it, soldier!"

September 25, 2015 was the Muslim festival of Eid. Akhlaq's
family made a traditional feast of goat dishes. Some meat was
left over and stored in the fridge. Three days later, on the night
of September 28, the family was home, chatting after dinner. Unknown to the family, a dangerous rumor had circulated
through the village: a young man from the village told others
that he saw Akhlaq and Danish disposing of the remains of a
slain cow. Two men from the village got the priest to announce
from the temple loudspeaker that Akhlaq had killed a cow and
his family was eating beef. A crowd of about 200 people gathered near the temple and marched to Akhlaq's house. "I heard
the noise and stepped out to check what it was," Danish told me.

54   "I saw a huge crowd outside our gate." He heard someone shout, "That is him. Akhlaq's son!"

Danish saw the men pound the gate; some of them began trying to climb over it. He ran back inside and led his parents, his sister, and his grandmother up the stairs to a room on the first floor. "We bolted the door from inside," Danish recalled. "We didn't even know why they were attacking us." The mob followed them up the stairs and forced open the door. A few men dragged Akhlaq down the stairs. Before Danish could react, someone hit him with a brick on his head. More blows came. His skull opened up and blood gushed over his face.

On the narrow street outside their house, the mob pounded Akhlaq with fists, boots, and bricks. A little later, police arrived and pulled him away from the mob. They moved the bleeding father and son to a hospital. Akhlaq died on a bed beside his son. "He was gone when I came to my senses," Danish told me. As he spoke, his hand involuntarily touched the left side of his temple, where a thick scar and a depression marked where doctors removed part of his broken frontal temporal bone.

After the lynching, the Indian Air Force transferred Sartaj to Delhi. The family locked their home in Bishara and left for good. "We couldn't live there anymore," Sartaj told me. "We won't go back ever." They moved into an Air Force base on the southern edge of Delhi, where he was allotted a neat, tiny apartment with two rooms and a kitchen. Sartaj shared it with his grandmother, sister, brother, wife, and his four-year-old daughter. It was cramped, but the base was ordered, quiet, and safe. Danish refused to leave the heavily fortified and patrolled base. "He gets angry, he gets irritated quickly," Sartaj told me. He

hoped that maybe after a year, and another surgery, his brother
could return to study and try again to make a life.

Government labs had conducted tests on the meat found in
their refrigerator in Bishara. A report had confirmed it was mut-
ton and not beef. Sartaj walked me out. I tried to say something
reassuring. He smiled a sad smile. "We will live with a certain
emptiness."

The emptiness was stark in the alley outside his lost home
in Bishara. A neighbor helped me take a look at Sartaj's locked
home from his roof. "The villagers will be angry if you walk to
their house," the neighbor told me. An investigation into the
lynching continues; several young men had been arrested,
including the son of a local BJP leader. But at best it would be
years before anyone would be sentenced.

Some of the Muslim families in the village had stayed. I
walked across the village to the storefront mosque. Men and
women outside their homes stared nervously. A few policemen
were posted outside the mosque. Five men and four young boys
were praying. After the prayers, the kids ran around in the dusty
courtyard. I sat with the men on a wooden bed on the mosque
roof. Two of them were masons; two were farmhands. They
worked for the village Hindus. "Where would we go? We can't
afford to buy a house anywhere else," an older man said. "Here,
we have our homes. And the village is quiet now. Things are better." A young man, who had wrapped himself in a blanket and sat
on the floor, raised his head. "There is one difference in living
here now," he said. "In the old days, if I had an argument I would
retort. Now I bow my head and keep walking."

The Country Without a Post Office

On an August 2015 morning, two young men on a motorcycle stopped outside the home of Malleshappa Kalburgi, a 78-year-old literature scholar in the town of Dharwad in the southern state of Karnataka. One rider stayed on the bike while the other walked up to Kalburgi's door and introduced himself as a former student. Kalburgi had been the vice-chancellor of Kannada University, and he was famous for his critique of superstition and conservative practices, which angered Hindu extremists. After a brief conversation, the "student" fired at Kalburgi with a pistol, hitting him in the chest and forehead, and escaped on the waiting motorcycle.

The assassination of Kalburgi was the third murder of an Indian intellectual in two years. In February 2015, Govind Pansare, an 81-year-old Communist politician and writer, was entering his house after a morning walk with his wife in

Kolhapur town in western state of Maharashtra. Two men on a motorbike, their faces covered with stoles, stopped on the street and repeatedly shot him with a pistol. He died in a hospital four days later. In August 2013, Narendra Dabholkar, a 67-year-old doctor and rationalist thinker who like Kalburgi had campaigned against superstition and black magic for decades, was on his morning walk in Pune, a few hours from Pansare's home, when two men shot him point-blank and escaped on a motorbike. After Dhabolkar's murder, an anonymous letter had threatened Pansare. "You will meet the fate of Dhabolkar," it had said.

Uday Prakash, a 65-year-old writer who is one of India's finest novelists, was in Anuppur, his village in the central Indian state of Madhya Pradesh, when he heard of Kalburgi's killing. Prakash had recently arrived from a suburb of Delhi, where he spends half his time. The talk in Delhi about the nation's booming economy, Modi's plans to turn India into a manufacturing hub, and building "smart cities" all over the country grated on him. A famine was raging through hundreds of villages.

Most villagers are subsistence farmers who depend on a single crop—rice. The harvest that year had failed. Prakash knew that desperate poverty first hand. He had left his village as a teenager after his parents died and worked as a construction worker, a farmhand, and an errand boy, all the while educating himself, eventually becoming a journalist and writer in Delhi. Years later, after he found literary success, he had returned home and began living there for a few months of the year. "All around me people didn't have food to eat," Prakash said. His village is near the border of the state of Chattisgarh, where a Maoist-led insurgency has been raging for several years. Prakash said that

58   sympathy toward the poor gets a person branded as a "Maoist terrorist." "I was living with a feeling that borders are being created everywhere in the country," he told me. Since Modi came to power, Prakash had been feeling fearful, as if India had undergone a societal shift. Kalburgi's murder was the third Indian intellectual in two years, and it rattled him. "India has always had riots, but the targeted killings of intellectuals and dissidents is a new thing," he said.

He called a fellow writer to speak about the murder, and his friend had reached out to the academy of letters and found it hadn't even sent a message of condolences to Kalburgi's family. "Sahitya Akademi Awards are supposedly given to a writer to honor him for outstanding work. It is an award I had received. One of us is killed and they don't even say a word," Prakash recalled.

"For a while now, writers, artists, thinkers, and intellectuals in our country have faced violent, insulting behavior," Prakash posted on his Facebook page. "This is not the time to stay silent, seal our lips, and hide in safety somewhere. If we choose that, it is going to get more dangerous. In protest against the murder of Mr. Kalburgi, with humility, and with great concern I return the Sahitya Akademi Award granted to me in 2010—11 for my novel *Mohandas*. I am in my village at the moment. I will reach Delhi by September 6—7 and will return my award certificate and prize money."

The Hindi language newspapers, which sell tens of millions of copies and mostly lean right, greeted his decision with mostly silence and some derision. The liberal English press interviewed him. A month passed. Mohammad Akhlaq was lynched to death in Bishara village outside Delhi. India had reached a tipping point.

Nayantara Sahgal, an 88-year-old novelist and essayist who had won the national academy award for her novel *Rich Like Us* in 1986, and whose uncle, India's first prime minister Jawaharlal Nehru, had established the Sahitya Akademi in 1954, decided to follow Prakash's example and returned her Akademi prize. "The Prime Minister remains silent about this reign of terror," she wrote in a statement she titled "The Unmaking of India." "We must assume he dares not alienate evildoers who support his ideology."

A dam of reticence and fear broke. In a few weeks, five writers on the board of the Akademi resigned; 35 writers from across India returned their awards in protest against a growing climate of intolerance.

Jawaharlal Nehru University in New Delhi is traditionally known as one of the most open spaces in India, a leftist stronghold where one could safely debate sensitive subjects. In February 2016, I received a message from a graduate student there, Umar Khalid, inviting me to speak at JNU about the question of Kashmir. "We intend to take the debate forward on these questions of occupation and the history of it, the atrocities and most importantly the question of self-determination," Khalid wrote. I grew up with the war in Kashmir, reported on it, and wrote my first book about it. But I was traveling for work, and promised to speak on another occasion.

The event, "The Country Without a Post Office," borrowed its name from the title of a poetry collection that many

60   consider the most influential literary work on Kashmir, written
      by the Kashmiri-American poet Agha Shahid Ali. To speak of
      Kashmiri independence is rare in India, as liberals and leftists
      stop at a measured critique of the rights violations by Indian
      troops in Kashmir, or offer a vague call for dialogue. Khalid and
      eight other student-organizers were among a minority trying to
      push the boundaries of national consensus.

      Students from Akhil Bharatiya Vidyarthi Parishad (ABVP),
      or All India Student Council, the student wing of the RSS, had
      complained that the event was "harmful to the campus's atmo-
      sphere." University officials agreed and revoked permission.
      Organizers ignored the ban and proceeded with the program. On
      the evening of February 9, a small group gathered outside a uni-
      versity dorm for the event. Participants were reading poems and
      singing songs when members of the ABVP arrived. "Kashmir is
      ours, all of it!" some chanted.

      Several Kashmiri students were in the gathering, and they
      responded with a traditional Kashmiri slogan for independence:
      "What do we seek? Freedom!" Other protesters covered their
      faces with handkerchiefs, as if tear gas were filling the streets, as
      they often do back home. Someone yelled: "The battle will con-
      tinue till India disintegrates!" A scuffle erupted between the two
      groups, but after a while, everyone dispersed. "I didn't give it
      much thought. Angry political arguments happen here," a grad-
      uate student told me. "I went to the library, worked a few hours."

      The morning after passed peacefully. In the afternoon,
      Mahesh Giri, a BJP member of Parliament, filed a complaint at
      a Delhi police station, describing the previous night's events as
      seditious and anti-national activities. That night, Khalid and

Kanhaiya Kumar, the president of JNU student's union, agreed to appear on television as panelists on debate shows. Between 9:00 and 11:00 every night, almost every network exploded into a cacophony of arguing voices.

Kumar appeared on India News, a Hindu-language network. Deepak Chaurasia, a veteran anchor, appeared to be furious and repeatedly shouted at Kumar, accusing him of being a sympathizer of terrorists and an anti-national. "Do students come to JNU to study or to support terrorism?" he asked.

Khalid appeared on *The Newshour*, whose frothing-at-the mouth anchor and editor-in-chief, Arnab Goswami, played the role of a fearless patriot waging a war against India's real and imagined enemies. A caption in large font describes the show as "Super Primetime." The subject of his choice for the evening is called "The Burning Question," and computer-generated flames leap around the phrase on the television screen. Goswami berates and humiliates guests who disagree with him or whose answers fail to satisfy the questions he asks on the behalf of "The Nation" with his trademark line, "The Nation wants to know..." "He is the 'Nation' personified, and the 'Nation' is in a permanent state of murderous rage," according to one critic.

"You are more dangerous for this country than Maoist terrorists!" Goswami shouted at Khalid. Goswami then began talking solemnly about Hanumanthappa Koppad, an Indian soldier who had been rescued from an avalanche at the Siachen Glacier in northern Kashmir at about 6,000 meters above sea level. Since 1984 India and Pakistan have been fighting over Siachen, a 47-mile-long slow-moving river of ice circled by stunning peaks where air is so thin that soldiers posted there

62   live with fainting spells and intense headaches, lose their limbs to frostbite, and are killed more frequently by snow avalanches than by enemy bullets. It is a refrigerated no man's land which has cost India and Pakistan billion of dollars and the lives of several thousand soldiers.

"We are proud of him and we are ashamed of these anti-nationals," Goswami said. Khalid moved in his seat and began to speak, and Goswami went berserk. "You will not speak when I am speaking about someone like Lance Naik Hanumanthappa.... I have run out of patience with you, with the shallowness and half-literate nature of your arguments," Goswami shouted.

Some of the biggest television networks seemed to have declared a week of hysteria, hyper-nationalism, and Islamophobia. An anchor with India News egged on a spokes-man of the BJP to initiate police proceedings against the students. The lead anchor of Zee News declared: "We won't tolerate anyone insulting India. No traitor will be spared." Another BJP spokesman went on *The Newshour* with an iPad and declared that he was in possession of evidence of Kumar making a seditious speech, but the video on his tablet turned out to be doctored. (During another television debate, he displayed a picture that he said exhibited the obvious valor and sacrifice of Indian soldiers, but on closer inspection it turned out to be "Raising the Flag at Iowa Jima," the famed photo of six U.S. Marines taken by Joe Rosenthal in the final stretch of World War II, except the American flag had been replaced with the Indian one using Photoshop.)

By February 12, Rajnath Singh, the home minister of India and the second-most-powerful man in the Modi government, declared that he had directed the Delhi Police to take the "strongest possible" action against those who uttered Kashmiri independence slogans at JNU. A few hours later, Kumar was arrested on charges of sedition. Singh followed up by claiming that Hafiz Saeed, the head of the banned Pakistani terrorist organization *Lashkar-e-Taiba* (The Army of the Pure), which has a $10 million U.S. government bounty on his head, had lent his support to the students at the JNU event. His claims turned out to be based on a tweet from a fake Twitter handle that spelled Saeed's name incorrectly.

Kumar came from a working class family in Bihar, India's poorest state. His father, a subsistence farmer, has been paralyzed by illness for three years. His mother, a low-wage worker, earned $50 a month. An older brother, a worker in a factory in a distant northeastern state, pitched in to support the poor parents, who live in a small, dilapidated brick house. Beghusarai district, where Kumar grew up, has been a stronghold of left-wing politics. Scholarships had helped Kumar find his way from Beghusarai to New Delhi, and Kumar had joined the student wing of a leftist party at JNU.

Kumar was interrogated by the Delhi Police and kept in prison for three days, after which he was brought before a court in central Delhi. Journalists and supporters of his showed up, as did BJP politicians and a group of nationalist lawyers who chanted "traitors of the nation!" and "hail Mother India!" "Within seconds, I was surrounded by at least ten men in lawyers' coats," wrote Alok Singh, a reporter for *The Indian Express*. "They started slapping and punching me, targeting my face and head. I remember screaming at them, "I am a journalist. I am a journalist." But nobody seemed to care." A few photojournalists managed to capture a revealing photograph: Ameeq Jamie, a young activist from Kumar's party, lying on the street while O. P. Sharma, a BJP legislator in his fifties, stood over him and pounded Jamie with his fists. The police did not intervene.

Another three days passed until the next court appearance, and this time Kumar was the target. As he entered the court complex, another group of lawyers charged at him, punching and kicking him to the floor. One of the lawyers who attacked Kumar later walked into the courtroom and took a seat behind him. Kumar pointed him out to the police, but the man refused to identify himself. "Then he left and nobody said anything," Kumar recalled. "Police let him go."

The courthouse assaults and the tacit support by the Delhi Police stunned India. A few days later, about ten thousand students, professors, and activists marched through New Delhi to the Indian Parliament to protest the persecution of the students. Many wrote articles critiquing the violence.

Right-wing television networks began shifting their focus to Umar Khalid, who was also charged with sedition and had gone into hiding. They began building a portrait of Khalid as "the mastermind" with connections to Pakistani terrorist groups, providing "evidence" of the treason. "Call records accessed by the Delhi Police show that Umar Khalid has made calls to Kashmir, Bangladesh, and even West Asia," an anchor announced. News X, a struggling network, claimed it had an exclusive based on unnamed sources in the Intelligence Bureau that Umar Khalid was a sympathizer of Jaish-e-Mohammed, a banned Pakistani terrorist organization that has attacked India

and also participated in attacks against American troops in   65
Afghanistan. No evidence was offered in support of the claim.
One evening at a wedding in Delhi, I was talking to a friend about
the trial of Khalid. A burly man in an extravagant suit overheard
us, stopped in his tracks, and declared imperiously, "That Umar
Khalid! He is the man to get!"

Reports about Khalid's father also began to air. Syed
Qasim Rasool Ilyas was once a leader of the Students Islamic
Movement of India (SIMI). The student group had been founded
in 1977 at Aligarh Muslim University, a college about 100 miles
outside of Delhi that helped create an educated Muslim middle
class in India. SIMI was largely focused on the socio-economic
and political challenges facing India's Muslims. As a student at
the university, Ilyas had joined SIMI and risen to be its president. After getting his doctorate in chemistry, Ilyas retired from
SIMI in 1987.

A year later Khalid was born, and as he grew up Ilyas
resumed his activism. Ilyas became a spokesperson for the Babri
Masjid Action Committee, a coalition of politicians that argued
the Muslim case over who rightfully owned the land in Ayodhya
on which the medieval mosque stood, until a Hindu nationalist
mob demolished it in 1992.

Several members of SIMI, angry about the destruction of
the mosque and the massive anti-Muslim violence that followed, were radicalized at this time. In 2001, as the first Hindu
nationalist government ruled India, Lal Krishna Advani, who
fomented the Babri Masjid destruction and who had become
Deputy Prime Minister and Minister of Home Affairs, banned
SIMI. Federal officials argued that SIMI members had formed a

66   terrorist wing, Indian Mujahideen, which was responsible for a series of bomb blasts across India. Now, Ilyas's membership in SIMI, fourteen years before the group was banned, was being used in the trial of his son.

One afternoon I set out to meet Ilyas in Okhla, the largest Muslim ghetto in Delhi. An invisible border separated the upper-middle class neighborhood of New Friends Colony in south Delhi and the ghetto that spread out beyond it. The street turned narrower, the construction more frenzied and claustrophobic as I kept driving. The ghetto had witnessed building activity, often illegal but permitted by generous bribes to the police, because most Muslims wanted to live in the area; old personal networks and cultural affinity were partly the reason, but the big push came from the fear after the 2002 Gujarat riots. A squalid jumble of brick and concrete and dust rose around me for miles. The ghetto had no trees, no open public spaces. It housed a varied population of different educational backgrounds, aspirations, and economic circumstances, united solely by being co-religionists, who weren't allowed to rent or buy properties elsewhere in the city.

I met Ilyas in a modest apartment on a residential street. A billboard on the façade of the apartment announced it as the office of the Welfare Party of India; Ilyas is the national president of the party, which has almost no influence among India's Muslims. A few old men watched television and smoked cigarettes in the living room. Ilyas sat behind a desk cluttered with books and papers in a small room. He had been received threatening phone calls from Hindu nationalists. "Somebody even called from Australia this morning to threaten me with death,"

Ilyas said. His older daughter was a student at Amherst; a younger girl studied in Delhi. Modi supporters threatened them with rape on social media. "I can't even repeat to you what they have been saying to my daughters."

Ilyas is a practicing Muslim, but father and son embraced radically different visions of politics. After Khalid enrolled at JNU, his father saw him gravitating more toward broader human suffering rather than being focused on the problems of his inherited religious community. "He would argue with me that Muslims are only obsessed with their own problems in India. He wasn't ready to engage only with the Muslim problems," Ilyas told me. "How can someone who doesn't even believe in Muhammad be part of Jaish-e-Mohammed?"

The father appeared on television and appealed to his son to emerge from hiding and face the legal process. The police raided the homes of journalists his son had spoken to. A young reporter who had known Khalid since they were undergraduates, was interrogated for three days.

Meanwhile, to challenge accusations of being treasonous and anti-national, JNU professors were offering public lectures on the meanings of nationalism. Hundreds gathered when Gopal Guru, one of India's foremost political scientists, began his lecture with the question, "What is the nation?" "A nation has to be understood as the promises it makes to its people, and the aspiration it provides them. In 1947, we were promised a nation bereft of indignity, humiliation, and lies," Guru said. "And as I speak, we are seen as anti-nationals who are not fit to live in this country. The political class must be questioned on how far these aspirations have been delivered."

68   On February 21, Khalid and four other students emerged from hiding and congregated on the steps of the JNU's administrative block. Hundreds of students gathered to welcome them. Khalid was wiry thin and had dark circles around his sunken eyes as he stood on the administrative block stairs. He wore an oversized, striped crew neck sweater over a pair of denims. A carelessly wrapped stole around his neck completed the picture of a debonair campus radical. "Comrades, my name is Umar Khalid but I am not a terrorist," he addressed the gathering with a smile. Khalid recounted the charges against him, evoking laughter from the students. But the mood turned somber as he spoke about the threats of rape and acid attacks that were made against his sisters.

"For the last six years when I have been doing politics on this campus, I have never thought of myself as a Muslim, I have never projected myself as a Muslim. I believed that it is not only the Muslims but the Dalits and the tribals, too, who face oppression and prejudice in our society," he told the crowd. "The first time in seven years I felt I was a Muslim was in the last ten days." He repeated a sentence from the suicide note of Rohith Vemula, a Dalit scholar at a university in southern India who killed himself after he was expelled from the university following aggressive lobbying by a senior minister of Modi's government, who accused him of treasonous behavior and tagged him antinational: "I was reduced to my immediate identity."

The Brief and Wondrous Life of Rohith Vemula

On a late February afternoon, several thousand Dalit, leftist, and liberal students marched through central Delhi. A forest of hands held aloft posters and placards with a photograph of a slender, smiling young man with a curly mop of hair whose name was Rohith Vemula. Radhika, his 49-year-old mother, walked with the students, a modest shawl draped across her shoulders. Her large brown eyes were misty. "I see Rohith in all of you," she told the students.

Radhika had survived a violent, abusive marriage with a middle-caste man and raised her children alone, working as a tailor for about $50 a month. She had educated herself as she raised her family, eventually graduating from college. To get himself through college, Rohith Vemula had worked as a construction worker, made home deliveries for restaurants, and dropped advertising leaflets for stores. A college friend

70   described Vemula's life as "mostly about finding part-time jobs"
and "reading about science on the Internet." Vemula breezed
into a masters program, and two years later, earned a spot in the
science, technology, and society studies doctoral program at the
University of Hyderabad. He won a highly competitive national
scholarship, which gave him a stipend of about $450 a month.

To amplify their voice on campuses dominated by upper-
caste students, faculty, and administrators, a group of Dalit
graduate students at the university had founded the Ambedkar
Students Association in 1994. The group was named after B.
R. Ambedkar, the greatest Dalit leader of the twentieth century, who became the chief architect of the Indian constitution,
and ensured that affirmative action found a place in the laws of
the land. Affirmative action brought a degree of social mobil-
ity to the Dalits, but the inequalities, prejudices, and violence
of the caste system remained entrenched. Informed by their
experience of prejudice and the ideas of Ambedkar, the group
developed into a critical forum for the rights of the Dalit students, formed progressive positions on national debates, and
came into conflict with Hindu nationalist politics. Although
Modi's BJP and the Hindu nationalist mothership RSS co-opted
Dalit voters in several elections, these organizations continued
to be dominated by upper-caste men and held onto retrograde
positions unacceptable to younger, educated Dalit men like
Vemula.

Vemula, who wanted to be a science writer, spent his first
two years at the university with the Students Federation of
India, a moderate Marxist student group. Most of the Dalit
students at Hyderabad came from government-run schools,

where the medium of instruction was a vernacular language
called Telugu. They barely spoke any English. Their inexpen-
sive clothes set them apart from richer, upper-class students.
"Within a few weeks, our classroom would be divided between
the upper-class, urban students occupying the front rows and
the poorer, Dalit and tribal students sitting in the back of the
class. It is structural," Gummadi Prabhakar, a Dalit doctoral
student who had known Vemula, told me. "Our professors
never bothered to explain anything in our own language." In
November 2013, Madari Venkatesh, a Dalit scholar research-
ing "high energy materials" at the university, drank poison and
killed himself after his multiple requests for a doctoral committee and supervisor were ignored for months. A probe into his
death confirmed prejudice and neglect of lower-caste students.
Seven other Dalit students had committed suicide in the past
decade.

The experience of a largely segregated campus politicized Vemula, and he felt that other student groups were not
responding to the urgency of caste discrimination, so he
joined the Ambedkar Students Association. "Rohith was very
active and articulate," Prabhakar told me. "He wrote wall posters and pamphlets. Whenever there was a debate or a clash
with the right-wing students, Rohith would be there." Over
the years, the popularity of the Ambedkarite group grew; they
won student elections and grew more assertive. Vemula and
his friends, with their instinctive understanding of structural
injustices, extended support to other marginalized communities and expanded the debate beyond caste to speak out against
the continuation of the death penalty, rights abuses in

72 Indian-controlled Kashmir, violence against the tribals in central and southern India, and prejudice against Indian Muslims. Their positions pitted them against many Hindu nationalist students.

Modi's victory in 2014 had legitimized hate speech and physical aggression against real and perceived opponents. Words that couldn't be uttered at the dinner table were blared in the public sphere. Activists of the ABVP, the student wing of the RSS, backed by their seniors in the RSS and the BJP, displayed renewed aggression against critical voices on university campuses. In July 2015, a conflict between the ABVP, the student wing of the BJP, and Vemula's group escalated after the Dalit students protested against the capital punishment of Yaqub Memon, a Muslim convicted of being involved in bombings in Mumbai in 1993 as revenge against the killings of several hundred Muslims by Hindu nationalist mobs. A month later, students in Delhi University organized a screening of a film called *Muzaffarnagar Eventually*, which documented the role played by the BJP in the 2013 Muzaffarnagar riots. The ABVP rushed into the auditorium and stopped the screening. In Hyderabad, Vemula and his friends protested against the disruption. An argument with Hindu nationalists students on campus erupted.

Nandaram Susheel Kumar, a leader of the ABVP at the university, filed a police complaint accusing the Dalit student group of assaulting him. A medical examination disproved his charges. Kumar, whose brother is a leader of the BJP and whose mother was a BJP candidate for municipal elections in Hyderabad, took his complaint to Bandaru Dattatreya, a Parliament member and

labor minister in the Modi cabinet. Dattareya wrote a letter to
Smriti Irani, then education minister. "Hyderabad University,
Central University, located in Hyderabad has, in the recent past,
become a den of casteist, extremist, and anti-national politics,"
Dattareya wrote. "The purpose of my writing this letter is only
to highlight the affairs in Hyderabad University. I earnestly hope
under your dynamic leadership things will change in this campus for better." A few weeks later, Dattatreya followed up with a
second letter to Irani. According to *The Indian Express*, between
September and November officers from Irani's ministry sent
five letters to officials at the university seeking information on
the charges made by Dattatreya.

In September 2015, Irani appointed Appa Rao Podile, a professor specializing in plant disease control, as the University
of Hyderabad's vice-chancellor. Podile came from an influential upper-caste community of landlords in the state, and *The
Times of India* reported that Podile had close connections with
top leaders of the BJP. Podile also had a bitter history with Dalit
students. In the early 2000s, when he was the administrator
of the university's dorms, some Dalit students overstayed in
the residence halls after graduating from the university. "They
didn't have the money to rent a place as they looked for work,"
Prabhakar recalled. "Appa Rao Podile would raid the rooms of
Dalit students at 3:00 a.m. and throw them out with their bags."
During a dispute over the running of student kitchens, an angry
Dalit student slapped Podile in the face. Ten Dalit students were
expelled from the university for two years.

In December, Podile announced that Rohith Vemula and
four other Dalit students were suspended. Vemula responded

74 by writing a sarcastic letter to Podile suggesting ways to contain the growing political activism among Dalit students. "Please serve 10 mg Sodium Azide [a highly potent poison] to all the Dalit students at the time of admission. With direction to use when they feel like reading Ambedkar." Vemula's second suggestion sought another accessory for suicide, "Supply a nice rope to the rooms of all Dalit students…"

On January 3, Vemula and his friends were barred from entering most university administrative buildings and student dorms, participating in campus politics, and eating in hostel mess. Their rooms were locked. In a photograph capturing the banishment, three Dalit students are walking, carrying their cotton mattresses, a few bags, and a large portrait of their great leader B. R. Ambedkar. Banishment from most of the university spaces carried the bitter echo of untouchability, when Dalits were not allowed to drink from common wells, enter temples, eat in restaurants, or live within the boundaries of a village.

The five suspended students slept in the courtyard of a small shopping complex by the university gates, which Vemula described as a "Dalit ghetto." University officials froze his stipend. Vemula, who had been sending most of his $450 monthly stipend to his mother, was living off loans from friends. His younger brother, Raja Vemula, a geologist by training, worked an entry-level job at a research institute in Hyderabad, where he made around $250 a month. He had rented a place in the city and moved their mother to the new home. A few days before his official banishment, Vemula visited his brother and mother. "Rohith was very clever. He could deal with any problem. But that day when I saw him, he said there was no hope of being able

to complete his PhD. He felt that they would not allow him to do
it. He talked about the case filed against him and the pressure
from the ABVP and the BJP," Raja told me. "That was his last day
with us. That was my last conversation with him."

On January 18, Vemula walked into a university dorm,
entered a friend's empty room, and hanged himself from the
ceiling fan with the blue flag of the Dalit movement. He left
behind a suicide note. "I always wanted to be a writer. A writer
of science, like Carl Sagan. At last, this is the only letter I am
getting to write." Vemula claimed sole responsibility for his suicide and requested his friends and enemies be left alone. Yet his
letter would be shown on the front pages of newspapers, prime
time television, social media, and even quoted during debates
in Parliament. "The value of a man was reduced to his immediate identity and nearest possibility. To a vote. To a number. To
a thing. Never was a man treated as a mind. As a glorious thing
made up of stardust. In every field, in studies, in streets, in politics, and in dying and living."

In the following weeks, Hindu nationalists fought pitched
battles in the public sphere, trying to disprove that Vemula
was a Dalit. Police began investigating his caste status. Sushma
Swaraj, India's foreign affairs minister, declared that Vemula
was not a Dalit because his father, who had left the family
when Vemula was an infant, came from a lower-middle caste of
stonecutters, which is labeled as Other Backward Class but is
technically not designated Dalit by the government. "We lived
like Dalits and they want to deny us that too," Raja told me,
recounting how Radhika, a Dalit, brought them up by herself.
"Our mother raised us, educated us. Nobody else cared."

Four days after Vemula's death, then education minister Smriti Irani organized a press conference to speak on the issue. She insisted that Vemula's suicide had no relationship with caste discrimination, that her letters to the university had followed standard procedure. "There has been a malicious attempt to ignite passion and present this as a caste battle. It is not." She even claimed that Vemula could have been saved but was deliberately allowed to die for political aims. "No one allowed a doctor near this child, to revive this child. Instead, his body was used as a political tool. No police were allowed till 6:30 the following morning. Who tried to help this child?" Modi tweeted a video of her speech to his 18.5 million followers with the Sanskrit words *"Satyamev Jayate"*—"Truth alone prevails." University doctors disputed the claim, saying that a doctor had arrived within four minutes of the discovery of Vemula's body, and by that time he was already dead.

Modi's social warriors refused to give up. I even noticed that Kashyap, the IT professional from Hyderabad whom I had met in the days after Modi's victory, was engaging in fierce arguments about Vemula's suicide on Twitter. He denied Vemula belonged to the lowest caste, and even suggested Vemula had converted to Christianity. "So a young 'scholar' who wanted to f**k Hindutava [Hindu nationalism] ended up f***ing himself."

Turkey

Part 2

Crescent on the Bosphorus

On May 2, 1999, Merve Safa Kavakçı, a 31-year-old newly elected lawmaker from Istanbul, was to take the oath of office in Parliament, having won a seat two weeks earlier as a member of Turkey's new Islamist party, the Virtue Party. The problem was that Kavakçı was among the few Turkish women in politics who wore a headscarf, and no woman had ever entered the Turkish Parliament in a headscarf before.

In those days, Turkish female lawmakers wore dress suits to Parliament. The army secretly warned President Suleyman Demirel that it might be forced to intervene if Kavakçı took oath wearing a headscarf. The leaders of her own party advised her against it, as they feared a coup. In the days before the oath ceremony the Turkish press, dominated by hardline secularists, heaped scorn and vitriol upon Kavakçı. Her marriage was discussed in news pages. Pitiless caricatures appeared in newspapers and magazines. Reporters showed up at her children's school; teachers asked her to temporarily refrain from bringing her daughter to school.

The lawmakers' names were called in alphabetical order. Midway through the ceremony, Kavakçı entered the central hall of the Grand National Assembly in a navy blue headscarf. As she took her place, 130 members of the ruling Democratic Left Party began banging their desks with their fists. They stared at her, rose from their seats, and for the next forty-five minutes repeated in unison: "*De Sheera! De Sheera!*" ("Get out! Get Out!") "Put this woman in her place," shouted Bülent Ecevit, the Prime Minister of Turkey and the leader of the Democratic Left Party. "I thought my heart would burst out of my chest," Kavakçı recalled.

Turkish public life and institutions were then dominated by an authoritarian, hardline secularism installed by Mustafa Kemal Atatürk, the general who established the modern Turkish republic in 1923 after his victorious battles against colonizing European powers. Atatürk was among a small group of military officers who were influenced by the French Jacobins' radical revolutionary politics and absence of qualms about using violence and centralized government forces to transform society, especially in the absence of religion. *Laiklik*, a derivative of the French *laicism*, or secularity, became the dominant civic religion. Unlike the American conception of secularism, Turkish secularism had little room for religious tolerance and pluralism.

Atatürk saw Islamic practices in Turkey as regressive, and believed Western modernity was the sole path for progress. He

80   established a constitutional republic, replaced Ottoman administrative structures with a powerful, centralized bureaucracy,
and embraced state-controlled industrialization. He promoted
a homogenized Turkish nationalism, which ignored the existence of ethnic groups such as the Kurds, the Alevis, and others.
He banned Sufi religious orders, replaced Arabic script with
the Latin alphabet, and banned traditional clothing like the fez
("an emblem of ignorance, negligence, fanaticism, and hatred of
progress and civilization") and the headscarf ("a piece of towel
or something like it").

After Atatürk's death in 1938, the military, the ruling party,
the judiciary, and the government bureaucracy—collectively
identifying themselves as "the guardians of the republic"—
calcified his ideas into a hardline secular orthodoxy with an
authoritarian character, known as Kemalism. But far from the
coastal urban center of Istanbul, the Kemalist social engineering
project failed to affect the rural, religious majority in the Turkish
heartland of Anatolia. Discontent brewed both among religious
Muslims and Kurds, whose very existence as an ethnic group
was denied in the formation of a mono-ethnic nation state.

The battle between secularists and religious Turks played
out over the next several decades. The Kemalists met their
first successful challenger in the person of Necmettin Erbakan,
an engineering professor who dominated Islamist politics in
Turkey between the 1970s and the 2000s. Erbakan blamed the
decline of Turkey on corrupting Western influences and sought
to replace the Kemalist system with a "just order" based on
Islam. Less a religious fanatic than a shrewd pragmatist, Erbakan
entered into two calculated alliances with hardline secularists,

who made him Deputy Prime Minister in 1973 and 1977. During that time he made sure his followers stayed away from the often-violent battles waged between young Marxists and militant right-wing nationalists. The military overthrew the government in a coup in 1980, and for the next three years the junta crushed militant leftist activists in a brutal crackdown. Tens of thousands were arrested. Torture and enforced disappearances were widespread. Turks across ideologies remember it as one of the darkest periods of their contemporary history.

While the Turkish left was neutralized, the Iranian Revolution in 1979 energized Islamist politics across the Middle East and Asia. Turkey's generals could feel the Islamist revolutionary winds blowing across the border from Iran, and the military junta sought to preserve order by offering concessions to religious Muslims. Turgut Özal, an economist who effectively used his professional expertise, his half-Kurdish ancestry, and his Muslim faith to form the Motherland Party and win the national elections of 1983, brought a certain normalcy to the nation by ridding the Kemalist economy of protectionism and being the first Turkish Prime Minister to go on the Hajj. To Turkey's religious masses, Özal showed another way of being Muslim. Merve Kavakçı was 15 when Özal was elected.

Kavakçı was born in Istanbul to an academic, pious Muslim couple. The family soon moved to eastern Turkey, where her mother Gulhan taught German and her father Yusuf Ziya Kavakçı taught theology and law at Erzurum University. In 1981, the junta issued a decree ordering female students and teachers to uncover their hair and remove their headscarves. Gulhan

82   resigned. "She was very sad when she came home," Merve's young sister Ravza recalled. "I still remember that university president's name."

The Kavakçıs returned to Istanbul. Gulhan began working in her brother's construction company and Yusuf practiced law. When Merve enrolled in medical school, she arrived in a headscarf on the first day of class and administrators turned her away. Some women dropped out or moved overseas to continue their studies, while others began wearing wigs to cover their hair and beat the system. Merve dropped out. "Go to Iran," she recalled secularists shouting at her on the street. Her father began searching for schools outside Turkey when a friend called from Texas with an offer: The Muslim community in Dallas was looking for an imam. He accepted.

Richardson, a suburban town of about 70,000 people, with a few thousand Asian and African-American families, welcomed the Kavakçıs. Ravza was the first student in a headscarf at Lloyd V. Berkner High School. She was pleasantly surprised by the American tolerance for her religious practices. She would try to leave school soon after the classes to reach home for afternoon prayers. The school principal inquired about her haste; she explained herself. He offered her a corner of his office. "I would pray in Mr. Clark's office! We were filled with immense gratitude toward America." Merve gave up medicine and studied computer science at the University of Texas in Dallas.

While the Kavakci sisters trained in Texas, the Soviet Union disintegrated and the Cold War ended. Turkey saw renewed contestations between the secularists and the Islamists, between the Turkish state and the Kurdish minority. The economy was

struggling. Turkish military had unleashed a new war of oppression upon the Kurds. Weak, struggling political coalitions were
grappling with running the country. To make matters worse,
President Özal died unexpectedly while in office in April 1993;
his wife claimed he was poisoned by lemonade. Merve graduated and returned to Istanbul a few months later.

The turmoil of Özal's death once again propelled Erbakan
to the forefront of Turkish politics, as his Welfare Party
won municipal elections in most major cities. A protégé of
Erbakan's, a young, brash footballer and businessman named
Recep Tayyip Erdoğan, from a rough, working-class district of
Istanbul, became mayor of the city. Merve, who had suffered
enough secularist headscarf bans, wanted to play her part in
winning political power for her much-ignored fellow religious
Turks, and gravitated towards the charismatic Erdoğan; she
joined the Welfare Party to run its foreign affairs and women's
wing. Ravza worked on the information technology team at the
Istanbul Municipality. A year later the Welfare Party emerged
as the single largest party during the general elections, and
Erbakan became prime minister. He sought a reversal of secular practices, tried to re-orient Turkey away from its Western
allies, began speaking of an "Islamic NATO," and blamed Jewish
people for the crusades and capitalism, calling for "the Jewish
bacteria" to be cured. The military had had enough and forced
Erbakan to resign after only a year in office. The staunchly secular constitutional court abolished his Welfare Party and banned
Erbakan from politics for five years. In December 1998, his followers launched the Virtue Party. Merve Kavakçı was chosen to
run for Parliament, and she won handily.

* * *

Faced with 130 angry lawmakers pounding their fists on their desks and shouting at her, Merve was whisked out of the Parliament building; she never took her oath of office. She was labeled an agent of Iran; President Süleyman Demirel called her an "agent provocateur." A prosecutor filed a case against her under the notorious Article 312 of the Turkish Penal Code for "inciting religious or racial hatred," which imposes a three-year term of imprisonment. It was the same article used to jail Erdoğan in 1997, when as mayor of Istanbul he publicly recited a poem which included the lines, "The mosques are our barracks, the domes our helmets..." Even though the poet, Ziya Gökalp, is considered the father of Turkish nationalism, and was a Kemalist and even anti-Islamist, Erdoğan's speech was ruled religiously provocative, and he had to forfeit his position as mayor, serve four months in jail, and was banned from politics for five years.

Two weeks after the aborted swearing-in ceremony, Merve was stripped of Turkish citizenship because she failed to inform the government that she had become an American citizen. She lost her parliamentary seat, and a few months later she left Turkey for the United States for a second time. Eventually the Constitutional Court dissolved the Virtue Party after finding it guilty of violating the secular spirit of the Turkish constitution. The ban triggered a split in the Turkish Islamist movement, which had been dominated by Erbakan for almost four decades. A younger, more moderate group of politicians led by Erdoğan and Abdullah Gül, a former economics professor, left Erbakan and founded the Justice and Development Party, or the AKP.

Erdoğan and Gül avoided overtly Islamist rhetoric and described
themselves as "conservative democrats" who supported the
free market and Turkey's membership in the European Union.
Secularists remained skeptical about their claims, fearing the
party was masking a hidden Islamic agenda.

In February 2001, a month after Erdoğan founded the AKP,
the economy collapsed. One-third of the GDP was wiped out.
For decades the economy had relied heavily on foreign investment, and the government ran up a huge debt that it in turn
relied on the banks to buy up. The government's inability to
establish stable political coalitions, its war with the Kurds,
and mounting corruption scandals caused foreign investors to
pull their funds over the years; when the crash came, a third of
Turkish banks went under.

The lone bright spot was the AKP, which had run its cities competently and was untainted by corruption. In 2002 the
party won the general elections with 32 percent of the vote. Gül
became prime minister, but Erdoğan, who was still ostensibly
banned from politics, was always the true leader. When Erdoğan
took over in 2003, he defied his critics by earnestly embrac-
ing Turkey's bid for the European Union, pushing democratic
reforms in order to start negotiations for accession, and following the guidelines of an IMF recovery package secured by his
predecessors. Foreign direct investment into Turkey returned.
Erdoğan placed great emphasis on infrastructure, and highways
expanded by thousands of miles. Turkish cities grew; office towers and apartment blocks became ubiquitous. Airports sprang
up even in small cities. Access to affordable public housing and
healthcare improved radically. Shopping malls, including one

86   with the Trump name, were being built in every Turkish city. The AKP's shopping mall culture also opened public spaces for a more diverse populace, welcoming among their customers both the secularist elite and the religious Turks, including headscarf-wearing women who were barred from universities and governmental buildings.

After five years in power, the AKP faced its most severe challenge from the old establishment—the military and the Kemalist Republican People's Party, or the CHP. In the spring of 2007, the AKP decided to nominate Abdullah Gül to the ceremonial post of the President. The CHP objected, raising the specter of Islamization by bringing up Gül's past in Islamist parties and his wife's headscarf, and boycotted national elections. The army website posted a note threatening to "make their position and stance abundantly clear as the absolute defenders of secularism." Turks called it the first "e-coup." As the military orchestrated massive demonstrations, Erdoğan simply refused to back down. "Erdoğan showed mettle as a politician. He stared back at the military and took the gamble. He went to the people with new elections, reminding them of his record in office," a Turkish economist told me. In the following general elections, the AKP won 47 percent of the votes to the CHP's 21 percent. Political scientist Omer Taspinar described it as "less a victory of Islam over secularism than a victory for the new democratic, pro-market, globally connected Turkey over the old authoritarian, statist, and introverted one." Nevertheless, Erdoğan had decisively crushed Kemalism, the dominant political philosophy of Turkey since 1923. The victory set the stage for the AKP to transform the country.

***

Turkey's negotiations to enter the European Union meant the
AKP had to improve the nation's abysmal record on minority
rights. A series of democratic reforms displaying commitment
to European Union values—while serving as a rebuff to Kemalist
taboos—followed. Erdoğan's Turkey saw greater integration
with European markets, although the accession process was to
turn into a long journey to nowhere because of Turkey's conflict
with Cyprus (which *was* granted EU membership), its inability to meet a range of economic and political conditions, and
the discomfort within Europe about admitting a large Muslim
nation into the fold. Despite official pronouncements, Turkey's
European dream has largely been halted since 2006.

Yet the EU accession process did cause the Erdoğan government to improve the lot of Turkey's oppressed and neglected
non-Muslim minorities. The Kemalist republic was threatened by ethnic minorities, who were seen as diluting the
nation's unity. The Kemalists resented that the merchants of
Istanbul were mostly Greeks, Armenians, and Jews, and sought
to establish an ethnic Turkish business elite. One of the most
disenfranchising acts of the Turkish republic was the promul-
gation of the 1935 Law on Foundations, which kept Jews, Greeks,
Armenians, and other minorities from buying and maintain-
ing land and property for houses of worship, schools, and other
buildings. Minority groups who formed a significant part of the
Istanbul merchant class, were also targeted with a wealth tax
that forced many to close their businesses and sell their properties. More than a thousand Christians and Jews failed to pay the

88   punitive tax and were deported to a labor camp. Most Greeks left the country after the Istanbul pogrom of 1955. A host of the remaining minority-owned properties were seized in 1980 after the military coup.

By the time the AKP came to power, barely a million Christians and Jews lived among Turkey's 80 million Muslims. Two synagogues and several churches are functioning in Istanbul, but these already tiny religious communities have shrunk further under prejudice and neglect. Erdoğan made incremental legal changes to restore the rights of Turkey's minority citizens. He repealed laws to allow minority foundations to receive grants from foreign countries with official permission; churches and synagogues were granted the legal status of "places of worship"; restrictions on minority community schools were eased; the Law on Foundations was modified to allow minorities to re-acquire properties that had been snatched and sold by the state. Turkey's record on equal citizenship for non-Muslim minority groups still requires a significant improvement. "It is not when you walk down the street. The prejudice shows in the dealings with the bureaucracy. When you say your name, they can tell you are Greek or Armeniain," Etyan Mahcupyan, a Turkish-Armenian intellectual, told me. "We have traditionally been the merchant class. We are very middle class but there are no Armenians or Greeks in the Turkish government or bureaucracy. Even if you applied you wouldn't be hired."

The biggest injustice that needed to be corrected was the one against the Kurds. The campaign of pacification carried out by the Turkish military in the 1990s was one of remorseless brutality. The army depopulated some 4,000 villages and burned down the forests of Eastern Anatolia to deprive the Kurdish guerillas of sanctuaries. Kurdish language was banned; identifying yourself as a Kurd was a crime. By the late 1990s, Turkey's Kurdish war had cost around 30,000 lives.

If the portrait of Atatürk hangs from every peg in cities and villages, the face that towers over the southeastern Kurdish region of Turkey is that of Abdullah Öcalan, the founder of the Kurdistan Workers' Party, or the PKK. In February 1999, Turkish commandoes—reportedly with American and Israeli help—captured Öcalan in Kenya. Öcalan was moved to İmralı, a small island about 80 miles southwest of Istanbul in the Sea of Marmara, and placed in solitary confinement in a tiny cell with a small yard, the aquatic expanse of the Marmara hidden from his sight by prison walls. For a decade, Öcalan was the only prisoner on İmralı—its most famous inmate before him had been Billy Hayes, the American drug peddler whose escape led to a bestselling book and the eponymous movie, *Midnight Express*.

The rise of the AKP—a political party that had always opposed the military—created the mood for a new tack on the Kurdish question. Erdoğan emerged as the politician who would go the furthest to speak to the Kurds. "The Kurdish problem is my problem," he said. Erdoğan lifted the ban on Kurdish language, and the Kurds were allowed to teach in their native tongue as well as set up radio and television networks. Peace with the Kurds could bring dividends: an end to a long war that would save billions of dollars; progress in negotiations with the EU; even votes for the AKP. Erdoğan and his administration

90   conducted negotiations with the jailed Öcalan, and in 2013 the
        PKK announced a ceasefire.

        That October, after 11 years in power, Erdoğan defied the
        last Kemalist taboo and officially lifed the ban on headscarves
        for women working in the Turkish government and other state
        institutions. "A dark time eventually comes to an end," Erdoğan
        said. "Headscarf-wearing women are full members of the
        republic, as well as those who do not wear it." A year later, the
        headscarf ban was removed for high school students as well. Yet
        there was still no woman with a headscarf in Parliament.

        In the meantime, Merve Kavakçı had earned a master's
        degree from Harvard, a doctorate from Howard University,
        and had taught at several east coast universities. In 2015 she
        returned home after sixteen years. She found a teaching posi-
        tion at Uskudar University, a small, private school in an
        upper-class neighborhood on the Asian side of Istanbul. The
        students played on their smartphones, and young women wore
        streaks of color in their flowing tresses, their stylish, colorful
        headscarves covering their hair. One could forget that a battle
        stretching over half a century had been waged over letting a girl
        wear a headscarf on a campus. The woman who had become the
        symbol of that battle was now grading undergraduate papers.

        A few flights of stairs led to me to a corridor lined with fac-
        ulty offices. Merve Kavakçı, Professor of Post-Colonial Studies,
        sat in a long, blue coat behind a neatly arranged desk. Now in
        her late forties, Kavakçı was excited over a new research proj-
        ect about the representation of footwear in the Turkish press.
        "We will attempt to answer how different practices of wearing
        shoes (wearing shoes/not wearing shoes in the house, or leaving

shoes in front of the door or not, or wearing slippers or not) are
represented in television series, literature, news and television
programs and how it can be analyzed within the self-coloniz-
ing arguments," the synopsis of "Putting Yourself in Someone's
Shoes" read.

I had grown up with the practice of leaving shoes outside
our home. Most of the billion-plus people in South Asia, be
they Hindus, Muslims, Sikhs, or Buddhists, did so. In Turkey,
however, taking one's shoes off had become a signifier of where
one stood on the secular-versus-religious divide. "The Turkish
press would write derogatorily about Erdoğan and his wife that
they take off their shoes when they enter their home," Kavakçı
said. "It was meant to show them as religious fanatics, people
who treated their homes like a mosque, who prayed at home, so
left the shoes outside."

The shoe was now on the other foot. Kavakçı's younger sister, Ravza, had also graduated with a doctorate from Howard
University, and she also returned home to join the AKP. One
evening the sisters visited Erdoğan, who told Ravza that she
should run for Parliament. Ravza was chosen as one of AKP's
parliamentary candidates for Istanbul and won.

On June 23, 2015, Ravza Kavakçı entered Parliament in a
long, blue coat. Merve had kept the navy-blue headscarf she
wore when she was kicked out of the same body in the summer
of 1999. Ravza wore it that day; twenty other female lawmakers
in headscarves joined her. "When I walk down the parliament,
they address me as Merve's sister," she told me when I met her
one afternoon last fall. "It took us sixteen years. Look, I am
standing here, in this parliament!"

The Feast of the Generals

On July 20, 2010, Recep Tayyip Erdoğan gave a nationally tele-vised speech to the AKP members of Parliament. Erdoğan is known for his menacing tone, but this afternoon he turned to poetry, as he had in 1997 when he was jailed for reciting what the courts considered an Islamist poem. But now he was in charge, and he used the occasion to talk about the notorious 1980 military coup that saw the junta murder young Turkish men across the political divide. Erdoğan spoke of Necdet Adalı, a 22-year-old leftist who was sentenced to death by the mili-tary three years after his arrest. The poet Nevzat Çelik's "The Dawn's Song" reimagined Adalı's last letter to his mother before his execution:

One morning, Mother, one morning   93
When you open the door to brush your pain away
Many of my peers
Whose names are different, whose voices are different
With flowers in their arms
Will a new country bloom.

Erdoğan cried as he recited the poem. The tears were designed to garner support for his next major political move, one targeted at the decades-long entrenchment of the unelected wings of the Turkish state: the military, the judiciary, and the bureaucracy, all of them long dominated by the Kemalist elite.

Erdoğan wanted to change the constitution, which had been written by the military after the coup. He planned a referendum on a broad package of 25 amendments which would reduce the jurisdiction of the military courts, empower civil courts, remove immunities for the generals who were behind the 1980 coup, strengthen data privacy laws, expand collective bargaining rights, and increase welfare provisions for children, the elderly, and the disabled. He scheduled the vote—a single yes or no for all 25 amendments—for September 12, 2010, the thirtieth anniversary of the 1980 coup.

One of the amendments in the package increased the number of judges in the country's powerful Constitutional Court from 11 to 17. The additional judges would be appointed by the president—who at the time was Abdullah Gül, Erdoğan's trusted right-hand man and the co-founder of the AKP—and approved by a majority vote in Parliament. Erdoğan claimed that

94   the move would democratize the highest court of the land, but opponents saw it as a court-packing plan to control the judiciary, which had supported the military and banned the Islamist predecessors of the AKP and various Kurdish parties. Breaking the Kemalist hegemony in the Constitutional Court would certainly remove the old threat of closure of the AKP for "violating" secular norms of the republic.

Erdoğan framed the referendum as settling the score with the military. On polling day, the amendments passed with 58 percent of the votes. Erdoğan had once again leveraged the support of the electorate to deal the Kemalists a decisive defeat.

The courts were to become a key ally to Erdoğan in his plan to chip away at the military's power and its interference in government and civil society. The old Kemalist junta was the target in two polarizing cases in Turkish courts that spanned eight tumultuous years between 2008 and 2016: the Ergenekon and the Sledgehammer trials.

In the summer of 2007, Turkish police found hand grenades in the house of a retired, low-ranking army officer in Istanbul. The seizure was followed by several waves of arrests encompassing more than 200 military officers, journalists, academics, and lawyers. More weapons, several computers, and hundreds of documents were seized. Turkish prosecutors alleged the documents revealed the existence of a hitherto unknown terrorist organization named Ergenekon—in Turkish legend, Ergenekon is the name of a mountain valley where the ancestors of the Turkic peoples were trapped, until a grey wolf appeared and showed them the way to the plains—which had plans to attack

newspapers, down Turkish planes, assassinate religious leaders, and create chaos in the buildup to a military coup against
the AKP government.

The list of men arrested and accused in the Ergenekon case
featured some names that haunted Turkish liberals and the
Kurdish population. Retired general Veli Küçük had founded
the Gendarmerie Intelligence Organization of the military,
which used disappearances, torture, and death squads in the war
against the Kurds in the 1990s. Sedat Peker was a flamboyant
mob boss who was also an ardent nationalist. Kemal Kerinçsiz,
a nationalist lawyer, was notorious for filing cases against writers and journalists (including Orhan Pamuk, Elif Shafak, and the
Turkish-Armenian editor Hrant Dink, who was murdered by a
17-year-old nationalist in 2007) for "insulting Turkishness."

The trial suggested that rogue elements of the old establishment could be held accountable for their crimes. "We
were initially excited about it," Emma Sinclair Webb, a senior
researcher with Human Rights Watch, told me. "It offered the
possibility that a group of military officers who were on trial
might be investigated for the enforced disappearances, torture, and evacuations of Kurdish villages." Family members of
Kurdish victims tried to attend the trials, but were turned away.
"Then we saw the trials weren't fair either, and they expanded
to include a very wide range of people," Webb said.

The police soon began arresting more people who opposed
Erdoğan and the AKP. A 73-year-old academic who founded
a charity to help educate poor, rural girls was arrested during a
chemotherapy session. Emin Sirin, a founding member of the
AKP who had fallen out with Erdoğan, was charged with being

96   a member of Ergenekon. Ergun Poyraz, whose book, *Children of Moses: Tayyip and Emine*, alleged that Erdoğan and his wife are secret Jews who rose to power as part of a Zionist conspiracy to undermine Turkish secularism, was also charged with being a member of Ergenekon. Mehmet Haberal, a surgeon who pioneered kidney transplants in Turkey, was accused to trying to mistreat then-prime minister Bülent Ecevit in 2002 when he was admitted for surgery to a hospital at Haberal's Bishkent University. The surgery had been successful; Ecevit had returned to work and lived years after that. Haberal was convicted of "founding and running a terrorist organization" along with Yalçın Küçük, a socialist writer, and İlhan Selçuk, retired editor of a prominent Kemalist newspaper. All of them were critics of the AKP. Haberal was sentenced to more than 12 years in prison. A group of scientists led by Nobel Laureate and MIT economist Peter Diamond visited Haberal in prison in 2013 and wrote in their report: "Dr. Haberal, who is 69 years old, looked pale, tired, and perplexed."

A British researcher named Gareth Jenkins took it upon himself to read through the indictments and evidence in the Ergenekon case. He concluded that "hundreds of pages of transcripts of wiretaps included in the two indictments contain no evidence even to suggest the existence of an organization called Ergenekon." Jenkins saw Ergenekon as the creation of a conspiracy theorist and argued that the absence of proof of Ergenekon's existence seemed to have reinforced the investigators' fear of "its awesome power and capacity for secrecy."

A growing number of arrests included critics of a Muslim preacher named Fethullah Gülen, himself alleged to head a vast, global network of followers collectively referred to as the

Gülenist Movement, who had over the years become a key ally of Erdoğan's. Ahmet Sik, a reporter with the left-liberal *Radikal* newspaper, was accused of being an Ergenekon member shortly before he was about to publish *The Imam's Army*, a book that investigated whether Gülenists had infiltrated Turkey's police force and its intelligence wing. Charged along with him was his colleague Nedem Sener, who worked at the *Milliyet*, and whose reporting into the murder of Hrant Dink had pointed fingers at members of the Turkish police.

Zaman and *Today's Zaman*, the most prominent newspapers in the Gülenist media empire, were the loudest cheerleaders of the Ergenekon trials. Andrew Finkel, a journalist who has reported from Turkey for some 30 years and a columnist for *Today's Zaman*, wrote an op-ed for *The New York Times* criticizing the arrest of Sik and Sener; he was fired from *Today's Zaman* soon after.

In 2013, 19 of the alleged leading co-conspirators of the supposed Ergenekon network were sentenced to life imprisonment; some 250 other defendants received prison terms of several years' length.

An idea had been taking hold that Gülen's followers had infiltrated the police and the courts, and in alliance with the AKP, they had managed to arrest and convict their enemies—ironically, by accusing them of being in a terrorist organization. A confidential 2009 cable from James Jeffrey, then U.S. Ambassador to Turkey (which became public as part of the Wikileaks trove), echoed the rumors. "Gülenists also reportedly dominate the Turkish National Police, where they serve as the vangard for the Ergenekon investigation," Jeffrey wrote. "The

98   assertion that the TNP is controlled by Gülenists is impossible
      to confirm but we have found no one who disputes it, and we
      have heard accounts that TNP applicants who stay at Gülenist
      pensions are provided the answers in advance to the TNP
      entrance exam."

Fethullah Gülen was born in 1941 in an Eastern Anatolian village. His father was an imam and his mother taught the Quran, although Islamic education was banned by the Kemalists. That didn't stop him from becoming an imam himself; by the 1970s, his charisma and oratory attracted a growing number of followers. Gülen propagated a mixture of moderate Islam, prosperity gospel, and Sufism that offered the alluring possibility of being Muslim, modern, and rich at the same time—a middle ground between authoritarian Kemalism and utopian Islamism. Tapes of his speeches circulated widely.

Gülen urged his followers to build dormitories in Turkish cities where rural students could find shelter and support for their careers. By the 1980s, after Turgut Özal's economic liberalization and easing of restrictions on Islam, the Gülen movement had created a vast network of schools—considered some of the best in Turkey—that provided secular education along with a course in religious studies. The education system requires students to pass an exam that determines his or her placement at a college or a university. Gülen built a chain of preparatory schools that helped thousands of students to score higher and get into the colleges of their choice. They also became the perfect recruitment grounds for the organization. "Despite what we think of them politically, we would tell our

relatives in the villages to send their children to Gülen schools,"
a Kurdish activist told me.

A decade later, Gülen-controlled businesses and schools had spread globally, from Tajiskistan to Australia, Brazil to Pakistan, Houston to Chicago, adding to his empire's soft power and connections with the elites of the host countries. In the early 2000s, as Erdoğan founded the AKP and positioned it as a party of globally minded conservative democrats, he found it wise to join hands with the Gülen movement.

By then the Gülenists had established an increasingly impressive number of universities, construction companies, television networks, and newspapers across Turkey. The global Gülen networks were of use to Turkish diplomats. The Gülen media companies championed the AKP and its policies. Together they undermined the old Kemalist order.

Gülen himself had been living in rural Pennsylvania since 1997, when he ostensibly traveled to the United States to treat a heart condition and diabetes. His critics believe he was avoiding prosecution by the secularist establishment. In 1999 a video surfaced that purportedly showed Gülen telling a group of his followers, "You must move in the arteries of the system, without anyone noticing your existence, until you reach all the power centers. You must wait until such time as you have gotten all the state power, until you have brought to your side all the power of the constitutional institutions in Turkey. Until then any step will be too early." Gulen claimed the video had been tampered with. The next year, he was charged with anti-secular activities and running a covert operation to undermine the integrity of the Turkish state. A Turkish court acquitted him in 2006, but

Gülen remained in Pennsylvania, communicating with his followers through online videos, web postings, and interviews with carefully chosen journalists. Hakan Yavuz, a professor at the University of Utah, estimated the number of Gülen followers to be around five million, but the Gülen movement has not revealed any numbers or a clear organizational structure. A strong sense of suspicion and wariness appears when you mention the Gülenists. An air of obfuscation and secrecy shrouds the movement despite its success. Joshua D. Hendricks, an American sociologist whose book, *Gülen*, is the best study of the movement, describes it as "strategic ambiguity." "Masters of spying!" a politician in Istanbul told me when I asked about the Gülenists.

The suspicion that the Gülen Movement used its sympathizers in the police, judiciary, and intelligence networks to persecute its critics and opponents strengthened over the next few years.

In January 2010, *Taraf*, an upstart newspaper patronized by the liberal intelligentsia, filled its front page with details of a 2003 coup plot, code-named Operation Sledgehammer, that was supposedly hatched by Turkish generals to overthrow the Erdoğan government. The military allegedly planned to destabilize the country and justify a coup by bombing the Fatih Mosque in Istanbul, downing a Turkish jet, and blaming it all on Greece. *Taraf* claimed that the mastermind of the coup was retired general Çetin Doğan, a dogmatic Kemalist and opponent of the AKP. Doğan had played a part in the imprisonment of Erdoğan in 1999. Doğan had also backed the forced resignation in 1997 of prime minister Necemuddin Erbakan, Erdoğan's mentor.

Doğan and hundreds of alleged co-conspirators were arrested and sent to prison. Erdoğan vouched for the veracity of the plot, and the pro-government press went after the generals. Gülenist media outlets were the loudest. Yet scant evidence was offered for the accusations, either by *Taraf* or by the prosecutors. Only six months after the arrest of Doğan did the court provide copies of the evidence to the general's lawyers.

Doğan's daughter, Pinar, and her husband, Dani Rodrik, both economists at Harvard, began investigating the hundreds of pages of documents. They discovered increasing evidence of forgery and fabrications.

The coup documents were supposedly saved and burned onto a CD in 2003. Pinar quickly found dozens of anachronisms that referenced names and events from years later, including a nationalist youth organization that wasn't founded until 2006. In one file, there was a mention of the pharmaceutical company *Yeni Recordati*, which wouldn't exist until the Turkish firm *Yeni Ilac* was taken over by the Italian group *Recordati* in 2008.

Encouraged by what they could find just through Google, Pinar and Rodrik hired a forensic consultant in Boston to examine the files. The expert turned to the key document of the trial, a Microsoft Word 97 document in Arial font titled "Operation Sledgehammer," with General Doğan's name under it, supposedly saved on a machine in December 2002 and burned onto a CD in March 2003. A tool called a hex editor was used to examine the file, and a reference to Calibri was found, a font that did not exist before mid-2006. Calibri references were all over the documents, and many were stamped with Cambria font, which was not designed until 2004. One Excel file was even saved in Calibri font. Pinar and Rodrik found that the documents were made using Office 2007, before they were ultimately saved in an earlier version of Office. What the forgers didn't realize was that Office 2007 creates metadata that is retained even when the file is saved in an earlier format.

Pinar and Rodrik had been publishing their findings on a blog and in publications like *Foreign Policy*. Rodrik published a long personal essay reconstructing the case and the forgeries called *The Plot Against the Generals.* "It was clear as daylight that 'Operation Sledgehammer' could not have been produced and burned onto a CD in 2003," he wrote. The two published a book describing their findings. A series of articles in *Today's Zaman* attacked Rodrik for disgracing Harvard, being a naïve son-in-law, and using his Jewish faith and connections to tar Turkey.

The judges ignored the evidence Pinar and Rodrik provided. In September 2012, the court found Doğan and more than 300 other defendants guilty of planning to overthrow the government. Doğan was sentenced to prison for twenty years.

Political currents have long decided the outcomes of disputes in Turkey. Between 2011 and 2013, the decade-long alliance between Erdoğan and Gülen began to fray. Turkey watched Erdoğan's AKP and the Gülen network turn bitter foes in a public divorce. The glue of resentment against the old Kemalist establishment couldn't bind them together after the successful subjugation of the military through the Ergenekon and Sledgehammer plots. Erdoğan began distancing himself from the Gülenists during the last phase of the trials. Over the next few years, an intense battle raged between the Gülenists and Erdoğan: prosecutors affiliated with the Gülenists brought corruption charges against Erdoğan's close circle, and Erdoğan retaliated by purging Gülenists from the judiciary and the police.

The clash created opportunities for the courts to reconsider earlier decisions. On June 18, 2014, an Istanbul court released General Doğan and 229 others accused in the Sledgehammer trial. In April 2016, the highest appeals court of Turkey overturned the convictions of 275 people accused in the Ergenekon case—because the existence of Ergenekon could not even be proved.

I recently asked Dani Rodrik whether Gülen's alleged clandestine army of powerful followers were really to blame for the purge. "The Gülenists, or more accurately their sympathizers in the judiciary, police force, media, and some other state institutions were indeed the prime movers behind those sham trials," Rodrik said. "Today, the Gülen Movement remains the only group that still defends the legitimacy of the trials and refuses to acknowledge that the alleged coup plots were fictitious." But he placed the primary responsibility on Erdoğan and his party. "Erdoğan and his ministers ensured roadblocks to the trials were removed"—police and prosecutors who didn't follow orders were fired, judges who didn't ignore unfavorable evidence or quash appeals were replaced, and for years the government publicly supported the prosecutions—"until the split with Gülen happened."

A Strongman Grows in Ankara

One barometer of the political mood in Turkey is to count the number of policemen in riot gear on Istiklal Avenue, the main artery of Istanbul. The faces of the young men in black uniforms indicate the nature of the day's political gathering. They are tense and edgy if the Kurds, the Kemalists, or another group critical of the government marches down the street. They are relaxed and chain-smoking if Turks waving national flags gather to protest the Russian bombing of Syria and shout, "Putin *Katil*! Putin murderer!"

On the afternoon of May 29, 2016, I was struck by the absence of the police and the unusual amount of festivity on Istiklal Avenue. Posters showing profiles of two men separated by five centuries were pasted together on the walls. On the first poster were the words, "We are celebrating the 563rd year of the conquest," and a picture of Sultan Mehmet II, who led the Ottoman army to victory against the Byzantine forces and conquered Constantinople on May 29, 1453. Sultan Mehmet, a figure revered by all Turks, was projected by the Kemalists in their own image as a man who knew Latin and Greek and appreciated Western art. The rise of the AKP and Erdoğan saw Sultan Mehmet's conversion into a great warrior of Islam. A Turkish company produced an epic movie about the conquest of Istanbul, *Fetih 1453*. The film and its trailers opened with a *hadith*, a saying attributed to the Prophet Muhammad: "One day Constantinople will be conquered. The commander who will conquer it will be a blessed commander."

On the Istiklal poster, Sultan Mehmet wore an ornate imperial dress and charged toward a shore on horseback, his eyes fixed on a prize. Below his picture, large red letters exhorted: *Rise Again!* The second poster, a few inches from the Sultan's image, repeated the exhortation: *Rise Again!* The face of President Recep Tayyip Erdoğan gazed purposefully into the distance. Mannequins of Ottoman soldiers with bows and arrows were placed along the street; an awkward group of Turkish young men were dressed in burgundy Ottoman uniforms. In another part of town, Turkey's recently appointed Prime Minister Binali Yıldırım called upon a massive crowd to "stand up with the spirit of the 1453 conquest and be united with President Recep Tayyip Erdoğan."

Scholars of Turkey have been marking milestones on Erdoğan's road to authoritarianism. Cengiz Çandar, an influential liberal writer who supported Erdoğan in the early years, saw the court packing of 2010 as a major signpost. "That was when Tayyip Erdoğan let it be known that he can do anything," Çandar

106 told me. In Erdoğan's third national election in 2011, where he handpicked the candidates for his party, Erdoğan's AKP won about 50 percent of the vote. The Arab Spring uprising was roiling the Middle East, and Erdoğan lent his support; the world talked about how Erdoğan's Turkish model, combining moderate Islam and market-friendly policies, was the path the Arab world should follow. "Erdoğan's ambitions went beyond Turkey. He was projecting himself as the leader of the larger Muslim world," Çandar told me. Erdoğan even spoke directly to the greater Muslim world in a speech after the elections. "Believe me, Sarajevo won today as much as Istanbul, Beirut won as much as Izmir, Damascus won as much as Ankara, Ramallah, Nablus, Jenin, the West Bank, Jerusalem won as much as Diyarbakır," Erdoğan declared.

Yet Erdoğan's bid to be a regional, even global, Islamic leader would be met with an Arab Spring-like challenge. It finally came when protesters gathered at Gezi Park and Taksim Square in 2013.

Taksim Square is a paved, open space at the end of Istiklal Avenue, encircled by the modernist Atatürk Cultural Center, the Marmara Hotel, an old church, and a Burger King. Nearby, Gezi Park, a small patch of green with a few rows of benches shaded by sycamore trees, is an oasis of relief from the bustle and crush of Istiklal Avenue. On most days, young couples, old men, middle class Istanbulites, and Syrian refugees all seek shelter there.

Erdoğan had risen to power at least partly by making construction and infrastructure a major focus of his leadership. In May 2013, the AKP government announced plans to tear down the trees in Gezi Park and replace them with an Ottoman-themed shopping mall. "In terms of scale and presumption, it would be as if Michael Bloomberg, New York's former mayor, tried to erect a five-story shopping mall in Bryant Park with façades like blinking Bloomberg terminals," wrote Suzy Hansen, an American writer based in Istanbul.

The decision touched a nerve, and a small group of environmentalists set up tents and began a peaceful protest to stop the demolition of the park. They were soon met by police in riot gear and bulldozers. That only intensified the support for the demonstrations, which by then had spilled into Taksim Square. Over the next two weeks the area and adjacent streets turned into a pungent battleground, as police burned down the tents and tear-gassed the protesters.

News and images of the violent eviction spread across social media, and discontent with Erdoğan found a voice. The demonstrations at Gezi Park resonated with many Turkish people; soon there were supporting protests across the country. Huge crowds gathered at Taksim Square, leading the police to withdraw. Protesters set up an Occupy-like camp there. The demonstrators defied Turkey's usual divisions between religious and secular. They included men and women of varying political inclinations and socio-economic backgrounds.

Erdoğan responded by announcing plans to demolish the Atatürk Cultural Center and replace it with a mosque at Taksim Square. "I won't seek the permission of a few looters in such decisions," he said. He threatened the protesters with mob violence. "We are barely holding our supporters—50 percent of this country—at home," he told reporters. Tens of thousands of his supporters responded, shouting: "Give us permission and we will crush Taksim."

Erdoğan had ensured a media blackout of his crackdown. CNN Turk, a television network owned by the Dogan Group, a media conglomerate which had been forced to pay hundreds of millions in taxes by Erdoğan, broadcast a documentary on penguins as the protests continued; another television network ran cooking shows. A small history magazine, *NTV Tarih*, dedicated a whole issue to the Gezi protests. Its owners refused to print the issue and shut down the magazine entirely. The editor Gursel Goncili decided to publish the issue online for free. The cover image of the last issue of the *NTV Tarih* was an Ottoman style miniature painting depicting the masked policeman of Taksim Square in Ottoman clothing pepper-spraying a woman in a floral red dress. Turks recognized the woman as Ceyda Sungur. On a late May afternoon, Sungur, a young academic at Istanbul Technical University, a few blocks from Taksim Square, had walked over in solidarity with the protesters. She wore a cotton red dress, a plain necklace, and hung a white tote bag on her right shoulder. An officer stepped out of a formation of riot police, crouched, and sprayed her face with tear gas from a few feet away. She turned her back to the policeman, who was wearing a gas mask, and he charged at her and sprayed her over her back. Sungur walked away gracefully. Osmal Orsul, a photojournalist with Reuters, captured the moment. Choking and gasping for breath, Sungur collapsed on a bench.

"The problem here was that Erdoğan was behaving like an old-fashioned, 1930s ruler. Doing everything, managing everything," the famed Turkish novelist Orhan Pamuk said in an interview with *The New Republic*. "The Taksim events were a good way of saying to Erdoğan, or to any future leader of Turkey,

or to anybody in this part of the world, that once a country gets
too rich and complex, the leader may think himself to be too
powerful. But individuals also feel powerful."

The Gezi Park protests became a rejection of authoritarian
and majoritarian politics, an insistence, as anthropologist Jenny
White put it, "that an elected government must also protect the
rights of the people who did not vote for them, the right of the
minorities, the rights of the people whose ideas or lifestyle the
electoral winners might not agree with."

Hande Sakarya, a freelance film editor, was in Taksim
Square when the police tear-gassed the protesters for the first
time. A tear gas shell exploded near her feet. "It felt like a revolution. All those days of protests felt like a euphoria, felt like
being in love," Sakarya told me. "The protests weren't just about
a park. Erdoğan always speaks in terms of his electoral majority
and ignores the plurality. His rhetoric makes people enemies of
each other. You can't go on ignoring the ethnic, religious, sex-
ual minorities. He is always on television, always telling us how
many children women should bear!"

After more than two months of demonstrations, Erdoğan
finally backed down from his plans to tear down Gezi Park,
though not before 11 people were killed and thousands were
injured during crackdowns. Gezi might not have translated into
a political formation, but it made an increasing number of Turks
think critically. After the media blackout of the protests and the
propaganda in the pro-government papers, Sakarya's father, a
fierce nationalist, revaluated his view of the Kurds. "He began
to talk about disappearances in the southeast in the 1990s.
He began saying how the press had lied to the Turks about the

110   Kurds," Sakarya told me. The ideals of equal citizenship and lib-
       eral democracy that Turkish citizens like Sakarya dream about
       have remained ever elusive.

       Turkey was still reeling from the aftermath of Gezi when a
       new crisis erupted—Erdoğan was falling out with his old ally
       Fetullah Gülen.

       One of the first significant triggers was the intense Turkish
       nationalism of the Gülen network, which meant they vehe-
       mently opposed Kurdish autonomy. Erdoğan's bid for Turkey
       to join the EU had prompted him to try to end the 30-year-long
       conflict with Kurdish insurgents, and over time he hoped the
       peace process would be a large part of his legacy. At the end of
       2012, Erdoğan announced that his administration was in nego-
       tiations with jailed Kurdish leader Abdullah Öcalan. By March,
       a ceasefire was hammered out, and the PKK withdrew all of its
       armed insurgents a month later.

       Whether Erdoğan truly believed in peace with the Kurds
       was to be seen, but far more important to his rise to power was
       his image as a pro-business, infrastructure-building tech-
       nocrat. He had especially trumpeted the highways, roads,
       hospitals, and tens of thousands of subsidized homes that he
       built in Istanbul and other Turkish cities. But a third bridge over
       the Bosphorus, which irked a lot of Istanbulites, was being con-
       structed at a cost of $2.5 billion; a new airport outside Istanbul
       went up for $14 billion. That December, an Istanbul prosecutor
       ordered a criminal investigation of dozens of people connected
       with the AKP. Among those arrested were the chief executive
       of the state owned Halkbank, a construction mogul, a mayor,

and and sons of three ministers in the Erdoğan government. Police raids found millions of dollars stacked in shoesboxes. Prosecutors and police were investigating real-estate corruption and illicit money transfers to Iran, and the three ministers whose sons were arrested were forced to resign. The Minister of Environment and Urban Planning suggested that Erdoğan himself should resign, as it was the prime minister who gave the nod to public construction plans. The corruption scandal was also reportedly tied to a money-laundering scheme involving an Azerbhaijani businessman accused of buying Iranian oil with Turkish gold to bypass American sanctions on Iran. An anonymous source released audio recordings that purportedly feature Erdoğan telling his son Bilal to quickly get rid of tens of millions of dollars supposedly made under the scheme. Erdoğan claimed the recordings were "montages" and dismissed the corruption charges as a plot by foreign forces and the Gülen network to discredit his government.

Three and a half months after the corruption scandal erupted, the AKP faced municipal elections. Although the charges had inflicted damage on Erdoğan's reputation, the AKP retained power thanks to support from a loyal base. After the election victory, Erdoğan accused Fetullah Gülen of orchestrating the scandal from America. "You know those people who used that blood-dripping, anger-inducing, hate-mongering headlines," he said during a victory speech. "Today, they have lost heavily again. Oh, Pennsylvania! Oh, the media who support them from here…"

Two months later, Turkish officials closed the graft probe. The Chief Public Prosecutor in Istanbul dropped the corruption and bribery charges against the accused, arguing that the evidence had not been collected properly and that there was insufficient evidence and no criminality. The millions seized in shoeboxes were returned with interest.

By 2014 Erdoğan had been prime minister since 2003. Although there is no official term limit for the position, the AKP itself decided to uphold a three-term limit for its leader, which meant that Erdoğan would have had to step down in 2015. Erdoğan, who retained good health at age 60, then set his eyes on the Turkish presidency, which would allow him to hold power for another ten years. Hitherto the president had been largely a figurehead chosen by Parliament, but Erdoğan was planning to hold Turkey's first direct presidential election in August.

The corruption charges had failed to discourage the AKP's dedicated base of pious Muslims, and a big chunk of far-right voters impressed by the strongman crossed over to embrace Erdoğan. Campaigning on a platform of increased prosperity, improved government services, and greater global importance for Turkey allowed Erdoğan to comfortably defeat his challenger, a retired diplomat.

A few weeks after his victory, President Erdoğan moved into Ak Saray (the White Palace), a presidential residence of more than 1,100 rooms in Ankara that Erdoğan built in a mixture of modernist and Seljuk architecture for $350 million. He even conveyed his Sultanesque self-image by dressing the presidential guard as warriors of past Turkic empires, from the Huns to the Ottomans, during a visit by Palestinian president Mahmoud

Abbas. The images of soldiers in strange, multi-colored cos-
tumes carrying spearsand wearing gold helmets were worthier
of a *Richard III* or *Macbeth* production.

With his power reestablished, Erdoğan wasted no time in
going after the Gülen network. Apart from increasing repres-
sion of the press in general, Erdoğan began specifically targeting
Zaman and *Samanyolu*, the Gülen movement flagship newspaper
and television network, both of which had turned from being
cheerleaders to bitter critics. In December 2014, police arrested
more than 20 people in raids on *Zaman* and *Samanyolu*. Ekram
Dumanli, the editor of *Zaman*, was briefly detained. Hidayet
Karaca, the head of *Samanyolu*, and the crew of a *Samanyolu* soap
opera that had depicted the government efforts to broker peace
with Kurdish rebels as an Iranian conspiracy, were sent to prison
and charged with "forming and leading a terrorist organization,"
ironically echoing the charges Gülenist prosecutors had leveled
against journalists during the Ergenekon and Sledgehammer
trials.

Every few months Erdoğan pricked the Gülenists, refering
to them as a parallel state, arresting journalists associated with
them, or seizing their properties and newspapers. On an October
2015 afternoon, I drove from central Istanbul to Bahçelievler, a
middle-class area near the Atatürk Airport. Bahçelievler is an
ugly suburb of glass-fronted tower blocks housing offices and
residential apartments, a monument to neoliberal excess. An
enormous building on a barren road housed the *Zaman* and
Zaman Today newspapers. Video cameras recorded every corner of the building. Bulent Kenes, the editor of *Zaman Today*,

114 recently arrested for tweets deemed insulting to President Erdoğan, had been released a few days earlier.

Kenes worked out of a minimalist office on a higher floor. Two framed posters stood on a sleek white cupboard behind his sparse desk. "Free Media Cannot be Silenced," one read. The other had a photograph of Kenes in a red check shirt holding a poster with the blue Twitter logo behind bars, and the words: "No let up in struggle for democracy." Kenes sat behind a bare desk in a dark jacket and a light blue shirt. Heavyset, with a clipped beard and restless eyes, Kenes looked like a hunted man.

After working his way up through several Turkish papers, Kenes, who is in his early fifties, was brought over from another Gülen paper to edit *Zaman Today* in early 2007. Owing to the scarcity of English-language news sources from Turkey, *Zaman Today* became an important venue.

Kenes edited *Zaman Today* through the constitutional amendments of 2010 and the Ergenekon and Sledgehammer trials. He tore into critics like the economist Dani Rodrik, and wrote spirited defenses of the trials in his paper and in foreign ones like *The Guardian*. "We supported the government throughout the EU process, through the constitutional amendments," Kenes told me. "We were with the AKP throughout the main struggle against the junta and the deep state." There was pride in his voice as he spoke of defeating the establishment. His imprisonment was a far cry from his days atop the media pyramid, when the AKP and the Gülen movement were allies in their battle against the military.

The social media warriors for Erdoğan's party are referred to as "AK trolls." "They threatened and abused me on Twitter, on email, on the phone," Kenes told me. During Ramadan in

2013, he got a call from the police informing him they had intelligence from a western Turkish province about a plot to kill him. His lawyers suggested accepting police protection. That night, he was alone in his apartment. A traffic ramp ran parallel to his apartment window. Around 11:30 p.m. a car drove slowly on the ramp. "Someone inside the car fired six shots at my window. I lied down on the floor till it was quiet and the car ran away," Kenes told me. "I don't think it was a coincidence."

Kenes continued running *Zaman Today* even after the split with the AKP. I read it regularly and followed Kenes on Twitter, where I was struck by the quantity and ferocity of his tweets. One day before the 2015 national elections, Kenes tweeted, "A thief, a liar shouldn't be a Prime Minister/President." Kenes was charged with insulting the president, which carried a sentence of up to four years in prison. (About 1,900 people have been charged with insulting Erdoğan between August 2014, when he became president, and March 2016, according to Turkish government figures.) In the first half of 2015, more than 50 percent of the requests Twitter received for removal of content from its site came from the Turkish government. On Facebook, only Modi's India, with 15 times the population, had more content removal requests than Erdoğan's Turkey.

Kenes was jailed for five days, and upon his release was barred from leaving Turkey and ordered to present himself at a police station every Sunday until his trial began. Kenes returned to edit *Zaman Today* the next morning, but he and his colleagues feared their paper might not survive long. "There is a rumor the government will take over *Zaman* and *Zaman Today*," Kenes told me. "Fuat Avni has tweeted about it."

Fuat Avni is a self-proclaimed whistleblower who has taken Turkey and Twitter by storm. He claims to be a man working in Erdoğan's inner circle, and tweets sensational goings-on and confidential plans of the government. Several of his predictions have come true, giving him a substantial degree of credence in the country's conspiratorial culture. Fuat Avni had tweeted about government plans to take over the Feza Media group, which published the *Zaman* dailies, Cihan News Agency, *Aksiyon* magazine, and the publishing house Zaman Kitap. He had mentioned other Gülen-affiliated targets: Koza Ipek Holdings, which owned gold mining, construction, and tourism businesses and ran *Bugen* newspaper and Bugen television network; and Samanyolu Broadcasting Group, which produces news and entertainment. Kenes believed in Fuat Avni's prophecy that Erdoğan planned to take over all of these groups, step by step.

The predictions of the Nostradamus of Turkish Twitter came true after a few months. On March 5, 2016, Turkish officials announced that they would appoint administrators to run *Zaman* and *Zaman Today*. Police fired tear gas and took over the building. *Zaman* produced a last defiant edition with a black front page and the headline: "Constitution is Dead." Abdul Hamid Bilgi, the editor, was immediately fired.

A few days after the takeover I tried to look up some old articles from the *Zaman* archives. A web page opened with the Turkish words, *Sayfa Bulunamadı*, or *Page Not Found*. Erdoğan's men had set out to erase any trace of the Gülen paper from the web.

A Shattered Peace

Recep Tayyip Erdoğan's contribution to peace and development in Turkey's Kurdish southeast is singular. Erdoğan's contribution to war and destruction of the Kurdish southeast is also singular. The chasm between these two realities is the very human story of hubris, failed expectations, nationalist anxieties, and the vengeance of a strongman. Between 2005 and 2014, Erdoğan continued a stuttering, flawed, but significant enagagement with the Kurdish national movement and its leaders. Throughout the years of peace Erdoğan took care to invest in the traditionally neglected Kurdish southeast. Diyarbakır, the largest Kurdish city in Turkey, transformed during the prosperity brought about by the Erdoğan years. Tens of thousands of slick apartment blocks, a series of shopping malls, Starbucks stores, and a variety of designer garments stores emerged in the newly built parts of the city.

But soon after Erdoğan assumed the presidency, the long engagement with the Kurds began to shatter.

In 2011, the Syrian Civil War erupted. Syrian Kurds, cousins of the PKK in Turkey, formed a militia called the People's Protection Units, or the YPG. The YPG had been administering Kobanî, a Syrian city of about 50,000 people adjacent to Turkey's southeastern Kurdish areas, when it was besieged by ISIS in the fall of 2014. ISIS had already captured hundreds of Kurdish villages nearby; hundreds of thousands of refugees fled. The lightly armed Kurdish fighters of Kobanî fought but the black banners of ISIS inched closer with every sunset; the fear of massacres that would follow an ISIS takeover increased with every sunrise.

Erdoğan saw the autonomous Kurdish canton of Rojava in and around Kobanî as an existential threat to Turkish sovereignty, a place whose existence fueled secessionist dreams in Turkey's Kurds, as well as a place of refuge for the PKK fighters. Hundreds of PKK soldiers fought alongside their YPG cousins against ISIS. At the same time, heavily armed Turkish soldiers and their tanks stood passively on the Turkish border a few miles away. The Turkish military even patrolled the border to prevent Kurds from crossing into Syria to fight ISIS.

Erdoğan also turned a blind eye to ISIS recruitment and passage through Turkey—it seemed he preferred an ISIS victory in Kobanî despite ISIS's threat to Turkey. Foreign fighters on their way to join ISIS entered Syria through Turkey with little scrutiny from Turkish security agencies. Based on evaluation of ISIS internal documents provided to the Associated

Press by a Syrian opposition newspaper, more than 3,000 ISIS
recruits entered Syria via Turkey.

Turkey's Kurds seethed with rage and burned government
buildings during a series of protests in October. Turkish police
and military fired tear gas, water cannons, and live bullets at
Kurdish protesters, killing 20. After the protests, Erdoğan told
a group of journalists that ISIS and the PKK should be treated
similarly, that "we need to handle them all together."

As American forces airdropped weapons and supplies to
the YPG and intensified airstrikes against ISIS, Erdoğan saw
that his bet on a Kurdish defeat was a bad one. He allowed
peshmerga fighters from Iraqi Kurdistan to cross through the
country to support the fight against ISIS, and Turkey housed
about 200,000 Kurdish refugees from areas around Kobanî. By
January, the fighters broke the siege of Kobanî.

Erdoğan's indifference to ISIS's attacks on Kurds cost him
goodwill he had earned over many years, but it had not yet
destroyed the peace process. On February 28, 2015, the AKP
and the HDP, a party formed in 2013 with the backing of jailed
Kurdish leader Abdullah Öcalan, announced the Dolmabahce
Agreement to end the decades-old conflict. Öcalan would ask
the PKK to disarm within three months, before Turks went to
the polls in June.

Apart from a desire to have the resolution of the Kurdish
question as part of his legacy, Erdoğan also needed the HDP's
parliamentary support to constitutionally transform the
Turkish government from a parliamentary to a presidential
system. A few years earlier, the Turkish paper *Milliyet* had

120   published minutes of a meeting between three Kurdish parliamentarians and Öcalan at İmralı prison, where they discussed the question of Kurdish parliamentary support for Erdoğan's executive plans. Öcalan had agreed to put Kurdish weight behind Erdoğan's presidency in return for a favorable resolution of the peace talks. Erdoğan needed to win 330 of the 550 seats in Parliament in order for the constitution to be amended and the executive plan implemented.

What Erdoğan had neglected was the political ambitions of the HDP's leader, Selahattin Demirtaş. A small, handsome man with a winning smile and soft eyes, Demirtaş was easygoing and funny, in stark contrast to Erdoğan's machishmo and menace. In a speech before Parliament, Demirtas boldly confronted Erdoğan. "Mr. Recep Tayyip Erdoğan, we won't let you be elected the president," Demirtaş said. "We won't let you be elected president. We won't let you be elected president," he repeated. It became immensely popular on social media, and Demirtaş went from being a politician fundamentally tied to the Kurdish cause to positioning himself as the challenger to Erdoğan.

The subsequent election campaign saw the further rise of Demirtaş as a political star. Demirtaş humanized his candidacy, inviting television crews inside his home as he spent a Sunday cooking with his wife and two children. On another network he broke into song and played the *saz*, a Turkish instrument. Younger Turkish voters warmed to him. Call your exes and ask them to vote for the HDP, Demirtaş asked the Turkish youth. The HDP nominated gays, Armenians, and Christians as candidates, which earned Demirtaş liberal support.

The AKP lost 9 percent of its votes, and fell to 255 seats in Parliament, far short of the majority it needed to rule. Erdoğan's dreams of an executive presidency were thwarted. Demirtaş's HDP received around 13 percent of the vote, winning 80 seats. Turkey's four political parties couldn't come to an agreement to form a coalition government, and Erdoğan called for snap elections to be held in November. More importantly, the polarizing campaign had meant certain death for the peace process.

On July 20, 2015, a mixed group of Kurdish and Turkish men and women took a bus from Istanbul to Suruç, a small town in the Kurdish southeast on Turkey's border with Syria. They were on their way to Kobanî to help rebuild the city, which had been largely destroyed in the battle with ISIS. As the activists gathered at a cultural center to speak to the press about their Kobanî plans, a young Turkish member of ISIS detonated a bag of explosives and killed more than 30 activists. Angry Kurds blamed Erdoğan and the AKP for allowing ISIS to fester in Turkish territory. A few days later, Kurdish militants claiming revenge killed two Turkish policemen. The government retaliated by bombing PKK bases in southeastern border regions and in the mountains of Iraq. It was the beginning of what's known as the Third Insurgency in the decades-long Turkey-PKK war, a wave of violence that saw hundreds of people killed.

During this time, television networks were broadcasting Erdoğan's blistering nationalist speeches and lengthy funerals of Turkish soldiers killed in the renewed hostilities. Demirtaş was being roasted for failing to stop the PKK violence. Grim reports came from Kurdish towns. The sense of fear, which the

Kurds in southeastern Turkey were long accustomed to, became palpable in Ankara and Istanbul. Reports came of nationlist mobs across Turkey attacking Kurdish men.

An impoverished Kurdish farmer's son from a village near Cizre in southeast Turkey, X had won a scholarship and graduated from an American Ivy League university. After graduation he returned to support his father and four younger siblings, working in Istanbul for a multinational corporation. I met him in the fall of 2015, and he told me that one evening in central Istanbul, he saw a few hundred activists of the far-right Nationalist Movement Party walking in his direction. They were demonstrating against Turkish military operations in his native southeast, which would have been in line with his stance. Yet what they chanted froze him with fear: "We don't want operations! We want a massacre!"

Turkish nationalism is a militant, intense force. Turks beat the Americans in the numbers of flags they fly on their buildings. Sweetshops in Istanbul sell Baklavas with a red Turkish flag and Ataturk toppings. X learned to avoid political conversations with colleagues. His father and siblings had to leave their home as Turkish forces went into the region to fight Kurdish militants. There were long days when he couldn't reach them, and he couldn't be sure of their safety. "The fighting has destroyed everything," he told me. "I am looking at graduate schools in America."

On the morning of October 10, 2015, two bombs targeting a leftist, Kurdish peace rally near a train station in central Ankara killed more than 100 people in the deadliest terror attack in the

history of modern Turkey. The Turkish government blamed
ISIS, and authorities identified one of the two suicide bombers
as the younger brother of the perpetrator of the Suruç attack.

That day I left my apartment and walked to Istiklal Avenue.
Everyone with a grievance in Istanbul assembled in front of
Galatasaray Licesi, a famed high school. The city's Kurds came
quietly in ones and twos and sat on the cobblestoned clearing
in front of the school. Slowly the numbers rose. What began
as a vigil turned into a protest, the demonstrators' angry, shrill
voices rising across Istiklal Avenue.

I couldn't understand most of what was said but I caught the
words *azadi* (freedom), *shaheed* (martyr), and *katil* (murderer).
The injury and rage were too familiar. One changes names of
places but the wounds remain the same. It felt like home, like
being in Kashmir in the 1990s. Tens of thousands of Kurdish
protesters filled Istiklal Avenue by the evening. The anger rose
with the energy of the crowd. Two slogans were repeated a thousand times: Murderer Erdoğan! Peace Now!

Twenty days later Turkey held its snap elections. I walked
around Istanbul with Ali, a Turkish friend. The morning was
pleasant, bright, and beautiful. The streets in Cihangir, our
central Istanbul neighborhood, were largely empty. Cihangir
had a mixture of old religious families and a large younger
crowd of artists, journalists, graphic designers, musicians,
and other young professionals. "The hipsters must be sleeping," Ali joked. "They will vote against Erdoğan but they will
vote in the afternoon." We continued down a steep street to

124 Tophane, a lower-middle-class area which traditionally voted for Erdoğan.

Recep Aksoy, a 55-year-old man from Tophane who runs a modest moving business with his two sons, had voted early that morning for the AKP candidate. A short, athletic man in an Irish cap, he wore a loose jacket over his baggy trousers and sneakers. "Let's have some tea and talk," Aksoy welcomed me into a *chay* shop. "I voted for the AKP but I have problems with them," he said. Three years earlier, his son had married and Aksoy bought him a small apartment with a bank loan. He was still paying back the bank. "But the interest rate has gone up from 0.8 percent to 1.3 percent and that has been hurting us. This is something they should have taken care of."

Yet he wasn't angry enough to have chosen an alternative to Erdoğan's party. I wondered if the glue of religious belief held them together. Aksoy laughed a short, dismissive laugh. "My sympathies lie with the Communist Party," he declared. The Communist Party of Turkey had split into two groups a year earlier; Aksoy was friendly with the Marxist-Leninist faction, which simply called itself the Communist Party. In the June 2015 elections, it had won 0.03 percent of Turkish votes and zero seats in the Turkish parliament. "They have no chance but if I have to do a packing job for them, I will charge them 100 lira instead of 200 lira."

Aksoy saw Erdoğan's AKP as the only party that could provide a stable government and reliable services. Before the AKP came to power, he had tried to get a license for his packing and moving business. "The bureaucrats those days treated poor people like me very badly," he recalled. "Erdoğan's government gave me a license, made me a legal businessman." Aksoy prospered during the first decade of the AKP rule but had been feeling the pinch in the last few years. His moving van was parked across the street. Aksoy is a regular at the tea shop by the AKP office and he spends his evenings there with his friends, mostly small businessmen. The day before the elections, he found no work till sunset. Some shopkeepers asked why he didn't buy anything.

Aksoy usually walked to the polling booth with his sons and wife. In the last elections, his sons had voted for the far-right Nationalist Movement Party, the MHP. Aksoy was annoyed with their choice. "I didn't tell them whom to vote for but this time they voted for the AKP." Aksoy and his sons were worried that voting for the MHP could lead to another hung Parliament and another period of chaos, which could hurt their finances. "Erdoğan is like us. He is from is from Kasimpasa!" Aksoy said, pointing vaguely toward the neighborhood a few miles away where Erdoğan grew up. "But we are all a little unhappy with Erdoğan. He has to cut interest rates and taxes. Money is our big worry," Aksoy told me.

The next evening the election results surprised most liberal observers of Turkey. Erdoğan's AKP had gained five million votes and won a comfortable majority in Parliament. The HDP lost a million votes, and the MHP lost two million. Economic anxieties, fear of chaos, and hope for better services and support from the government trumped any liberal concerns over authoritarianism, the shrinking freedom of the press, or the plight of ethnic minorities.

Many Turks and religious Kurds who had supported the HDP in the June elections returned to the AKP as the war

126   between the PKK and the Turkish forces escalated; they saw the HDP as enmeshed with the PKK. The ultranationalists moved from the MHP to the AKP, for Erdoğan had turned out to be a greater nationalist: the Turkish strongman who was crushing the treasonous Kurds. Two days after the AKP's electoral victory President Erdoğan reminded Turkey that he hadn't forgotten about the Kurds. Erdoğan announced his vow to fight the PKK until its last fighter was killed. "For whoever wants to make life unbearable for us, we will make life unbearable for them," he declared.

Journey to the Sun

On one of my first evenings in Istanbul last October I was a little disoriented and overwhelmed by my linguistic handicap in an energetic new city. In my hotel room, I gave up on cable television after I heard Jack Nicholson spouting fluent Turkish. Everything was dubbed; everything translated. My linguistic experience of South Asia, where colonization had turned the English language into a *lingua franca*, was of little use here. Turkish Twitter was in Turkish. I lay in my semi-dark, cramped room staring at the screen of my phone. Photographs of soap opera stars and politicians were trending.

A slightly dark photograph began appearing repeatedly. The photograph was shot on a cellphone camera after sunset in Sırṇak, a rebellious Kurdish town around a thousand miles from Istanbul, on Turkey's border with Syria. In the photograph, a black armored Turkish police car is driving through a dimly

128   lit street. Half the letters of a Turkish bank are visible from a
        billboard; a white car is parked in front of the bank; two blurry
        stores seem open for business. On the empty, cobbled street,
        the armored car is dragging the corpse of a man. The dead man is
        wearing dark colored trousers and a red shirt. His feet are bound
        together, his arms tied to his sides. A thick rope around his neck
        disappears into the back door of the police car. I found some
        tweets in English. The Kurds talked about the brutality of the
        Turkish forces; the Turks described the dead man as a PKK ter-
        rorist. The corpse of Sırnak conveyed the brutality of a Joseph
        Conrad story from a colonial outpost.

        A few months later, I met M, a young Kurdish researcher in
        Istanbul who worked part-time as a translator for journalists.
        I asked him about the photograph. "Haci!" M shouted, over-
        come by agitation, his face hardened by the memory. "You saw
        what they did to them!" The dead man in the photograph was
        Haci Lokman Birlik, a 29-year-old actor, filmmaker, and activ-
        ist from Sırnak. "I know his brother," M told me. "I will try to
        reach him."

        A few days after the photograph appeared, a video of Birlik's
        body was released on the Internet. Propagandists for the govern-
        ment had tried to dismiss the photograph as a fake, but the video
        suggested otherwise: An invisible policeman filmed it from the
        rear of the armored car driving on a desolate street. Birlik's body
        bobbed behind the armored car. His feet drew straight lines in
        the dust. Turkish Prime Minister Ahmet Davutoğlu ordered an
        investigation into the images, but not into the circumstances of
        Birlik's death or the desecration of his body. Davutoğlu insisted
        Birlik was a PKK terrorist who was killed while "attacking

the police with a rocket launcher." Turkish security officials explained in Turkish papers that Birlik's body was dragged through the streets because the policemen feared he might have been wearing a suicide vest.

On a November afternoon, I flew with M to Diyarbakır, the de facto capital of the southeastern Kurdish region. Diyarbakır spread over miles on a flat-topped plateau. Dark brown squares of sunbaked, harvested fields and distant rows of apartment blocks grew as the plane landed. The airport was a modern-ist cage of steel and glass built during the Erdoğan years. Thousands of apartment blocks in pastel colors rose along the smooth highway to the city. "The apartments came up in the last fifteen years," M said.

I checked into a hotel in Sur, the historic heart of Diyarbakır built upon a plateau overlooking the River Tigris. Grim, black walls of basalt built by the Byzantines circled the old city and reflected the mood. Dark green armored cars of the Turkish special police were parked by the black fortifications. In the afternoon, M and I followed a cobbled street leading to a bus-tling market by the medieval Great Mosque of Diyarbakır. Armed policemen in bulletproof vests stood on street corners. Old Kurdish men drank tea and talked in the courtyard of the black stone mosque.

We stepped into a street filled with kebab houses, tea shops, and spice merchants. The alley was quiet, a little edgy. It turned abruptly onto a desolate cobbled street lined with modest stone and brick houses. A boy ran past us; a woman in a hijab disap-peared into a house. It was eerily quiet. Graffiti on the walls celebrated Kurdish victories in Kobanî and Rojava.

130   A white tarpaulin curtained off the street. A pile of sandbags blocked the rest. A small trench had been dug in front of
the tarpaulin. "The barricades!" M said. I felt the fear in his
voice. He instinctively turned back, as if to check any police
movement. "An operation can happen there anytime." Under the
banner of the PKK's youth wing, the Patriotic Revolutionary
Youth Movement, known as the YDG-H, teenagers took over
numerous neighborhoods in Kurdish towns and cities in southeastern Turkey and ran them as "liberated zones." To keep the
Turkish forces at bay, the YDG-H had dug trenches in alleys
and put up barricades and bunkers to maintain control. They
planted landmines and bombs and attacked Turkish troops who
dared wander into these areas. In Turkish eyes, it was an echo of
Rojava, the autonomous Kurdish region in Syria, an unacceptable challenge to Turkish sovereignty. Erdoğan's retaliation was
merciless. Turkish troops closed off Kurdish towns and neighborhoods and shelled them to smithereens; curfew was the
Turkish euphemism for obiliteration.

        But for all the violence, it was the killing of Helin Şen, a
12-year-old girl, that had stunned Diyarbakır a month earlier.
"She was my first child, my clever girl," her mother, Nazmive
Şen, told me. She had a younger boy and a girl. Her husband
drove a taxi. Şen, a housewife in her mid-thirties who grew up
in Sur, found her neighborhood on the edge after the June 2015
elections. Nazmive delayed her grocery shopping for an hour or
two every time she heard a gunshot. "The curfews began after
Erdoğan lost," she said, adjusting her floral headscarf. "He was
punishing us for his loss." The third round of curfew in early
October, a few weeks before the November 2015 elections, was

four days long. She filled a small pool in their garden in anticipation of water shortage. On the first day of the curfew, her sick husband was hospitalized. She stayed in Sur with their three children. The fighting was so intense that she couldn't even walk half a block to a neighbor's house to get bread.

On the fifth day, Sur was calm. Nazmive bought fruit, vegetables, tomatoes, and oranges from a greengrocer. She returned home with her purchase. Jannat, her younger daughter, was sleeping; Kadir, her son, was sitting around. Someone mentioned the bakery had opened. "I had no bread," Nazmive recalled. Helin, her oldest, was in seventh grade. After the growing tensions, Nazimve had moved Helin to a school outside Sur. She had walked her to the new school for one day. The second day, the curfew began and the school was closed, so she brought Helin with her.

On the street, Helin was walking on her right; some female relatives were walking on the left. There were no men on the street. "Police suddenly opened fire," she recalled. "I didn't know what to do. I stood in the middle of the street in shock." A neighbor pulled Nazmive into her house. Nazmive woke up to Helin's absence and lunged toward the street. "I saw her lying in the street, in blood." Police were still shooting; her neighbors pulled Nazmive back. "I couldn't pick up my daughter's body." Her neighbors called for an ambulance, but nobody responded. "Helin was lying on the street for two hours," Nazmive told me. She didn't see Helin's body, her face before the burial. She couldn't bear it. "Those policemen had blood in their eyes," she told me. "I remember their eyes."

After Helin's death Nazmive and her family moved out of Sur to another neighborhood in Diyarbakır. Her husband Ekram

132   had sold his taxi and was struggling with depression. They lived
        in a modest two-bedroom apartment in the Baglar area, which
        had grown after the war in the 1990s had displaced more than
        two million Kurdish villagers. A few days after the burial, the
        police summoned Nazmive to testify about Helin's death. The
        police wanted her to sign papers saying YDG-H militants had
        killed her daughter. "They offered us money, told Ekram they
        would get him a job." Nazmive and Ekram refused.

           Although the Kurdish nationalist movement is dominated
        by Marxist ideas, a large number of Kurds are practicing Muslims.
        Nazmive sought consolation in religion. "Alhamdulillah, we are
        Muslim! We might not get justice in this world but in the next
        world, Helin's killer will have to account for it." Her eyelids had
        swollen from crying. She paused for a while. A bemused expres-
        sion appeared on her face. "You came from Istanbul?" she asked
        me. I nodded. She looked at me searchingly. "Will you write?
        Will you write all of this?"

        On a bright, quiet morning I left for Silvan, a town 50 miles
        northeast of Diyarbakır. The road followed the steep descents
        and elevations of plateaus rising and falling like waves between
        the two places. Immense expanses of rich, brown fields spread
        to reach the bright, azure horizon. Mulberry groves and tiny
        hamlets of pink and white houses appeared every few miles, as
        if a painter of stark landscapes had an afterthought to soften the
        texture of his canvas. The road was empty except for an occa-
        sional tractor or military truck. A range of low, barren hills rose
        in the distance. It was the land I had first imagined in the work
        of Yasar Kemal. "The rich earth yields a crop three times a year.

Each plant is huge. It is twice, three times, five times larger than in other soils. Even the colors of the flowers, of the brilliant green grasses, of the trees are different," Kemal wrote in his 1969 novel, *They Burn the Thistles*.

Silvan, a town of 90,000 people, announced itself with a row of yellow and white apartment blocks. A supermarket, a bank, and a pharmacy gave the town square a domesticated, everyday vibe. I noticed an outlet for Aygaz, the Turkish cooking gas provider, whose trucks announced their arrival with a nursery rhyme-style jingle. Pine trees grew outside the multi-floor Silvan municipal building, which dominated the scene. The HDP ran the municipality, which gave the Kurds some say in their daily lives, although the administrative heads of the provinces were not elected officials but governors appointed by Ankara. Those administrators controlled most of the finances and the security apparatus. Turkey had remained a state with a strong center.

After the collapse of the peace process, as the battles between Kurdish rebels and the Turkish military engulfed the towns and cities in southeastern Turkey, Kurdish mayors in scores of towns read out a declaration of autonomy—a symbolic rejection of Turkish authority, a sign of protest, and an implicit demand for greater federalism. Erdoğan saw the autonomy declarations as a sign of Kurdish separatism and responded by arresting several of the mayors. Most of the Kurdish-controlled municipalities had two co-mayors—a man and a woman— owing to the tradition of gender equality in the Kurdish national movement. Yuksel Bodakci and Melisah Teke, the mayors of Silvan, were arrested, and Turkish prosecutors were seeking life imprisonment for them.

The mayor's office was a large, bare room. A photograph of Bodakci hung on a wall. A sheaf of papers and a book were lying on the mayor's table as if the incumbent had just stepped out for coffee. A black swivel chair behind the large wooden table was empty. Kerem Canpolat, the acting mayor, a balding young man in a blue suit, sat with a few colleagues on low chairs in front of the mayoral table. "The mayor's chair belongs to Yuksel Bodakci," Canpolat told me. "I can't sit there while she is in prison." His words took me back to the ancient Sanskrit epic *Ramayana* and its protagonist, Rama, the prince of Ayodhya, who is exiled from his home for 14 years after machinations by his stepmother, who wants the royal throne for her son, Bharata. On being offered the throne, Bharata shocks his mother by placing the wooden sandals of Rama on the throne until he returns from his exile.

A short walk from the municipal building, a neighborhood of several hundred spacious but simply built homes presented a concrete picture of the nature of war. The streets were thick with wreckage of walls, roofs, windows, and doors shredded and blown apart by mortars and tanks. Cranes and bulldozers pulled at the debris. Workers gingerly picked up pieces of electric cables from mud; others stared wistfully at the burned, mangled electrical poles. The afternoon sun created tunnels of light through the holes bored into brick walls by thousands of bullets.

A young couple stood impassively on the porch of their house. Mortar shells had shredded the front wall; a subsequent fire had covered it in thick layers of soot. Mangled iron bars stood in burned windows. The living room was charred like a coal pit. They smiled helplessly. Another house, where Zozan Donmez lived with her husband and four children, had a wide

hole blown into a wall on the first floor. She had moved with her
family to her sister's house when the military began the siege
of Silvan. Kurdish fighters had taken refuge in her house while
they were away; she had returned a week later to a ruin. "Some
trees were being cut at Gezi Park in Istanbul and thousands of
people came out on streets," Donmez said. "In Turkey, when
a tree is attacked, people come out. But our lives here have no
value. They destroyed our trees, our homes, our everything."

Every element of domesticity had been broken, burnt, vio-
lated, and the loss of everything she had collected and built
over the decades welled up old, suppressed memories. Donmez,
who is a pious Muslim, turned stiff and spoke about something
she hadn't spoken about for decades. "My grandfather was an
Armenian. He was converted to Islam in 1915," she said. "He
was a little boy, his parents were killed, and somebody adopted
and raised him as a Muslim." Turkey brimmed with such secret
histories. The Armenian boy grew up as a Kurdish Muslim man
and his son—Donmez's father—inherited the political legacies
and traumas of the Kurds—another ethnic group battered by
Atatürk's republic. "A long time ago, my father was in his village.
His house was also burnt down by the army after they said he
and the villagers supported the PKK," Donmez said. "This is the
third time they have attacked our home." She spread her hands
plaintively, as if in prayer. "I don't think my children will accept
the same oppression." Donmez slowly turned away and began
picking up shards of broken glass.

The military assault on Silvan had been remorseless, echoing the famous phrase of Tacitus, "They make a desert and call
it peace."

136   Diyarbakır is a city between war and peace, between the casbah and the suburb. I was on my way back to the hotel after spending a morning in a shopping mall full of branded outlet such as Colins, Yves Rocher, and Starbucks in a newly affluent part of city when M called and told me that Haci Lokman Birlik's brother was here.

Mehmet Birlik, a tall, imposing man, sat toward the back in a popular restaurant. His faded denim shirt, camera bag, and careless gray hair lent him the air of a wildlife photographer from the movies. "Haci!" Birlik rubbed his face with his hands and took a deep breath. "The war began too early for him."

Haci was the youngest of six siblings, born in 1986 in Şırnak. Their father worked for the local public health department. When Haci was six years old, the Turkish military massacred 50 people in the town. "They rained such intense destruction on the town of Şırnak in August 1992 that all but two or three thousand of the town's 35,000 inhabitants reportedly piled their belongings onto wagons and trucks and abandoned the town," a report by Human Rights Watch read.

The Birliks moved to Mersin, a port city on the Mediterranean coast of southern Turkey, about 500 miles from Şırnak. They lived in a rented house near the Mersin shore, which attracted large gatherings of townsfolk. A displaced family from Hakkari, a town near Iranian and Syrian border, lived in a shop next door. A scuffle occurred on the crowded boulevard nearby; police opened fire. Haci was playing outside; a girl from the Hakkari family took him inside their home. They were trembling. "She later told us that Haci began consoling them and telling them that what happened in Şırnak was much worse," Birlik recalled.

In 1995, after three years in Mersin, they returned home to Şırnak. Birlik stopped studying after high school and ran a café. Turkey has compulsory military service, which begins at twenty for men who have not graduated from college. The Kurds resent the service, and Haci enrolled in an undergraduate program to delay it. In the following years, Haci got involved in ecological and trade union activism and emerged as a popular organizer for the Kurdish cause. In 2009, during municipal elections, Haci helped organize a rally of about 10,000 people in Şırnak for the main pro-Kurdish party, which led him to a seat on the Şırnak city council. Unfortunately, soon after that thousands of Kurdish activists and politicians were arrested and accused of being members of an umbrella organization with links to the PKK. The number of people arrested was much greater than the prisons could accommodate, so they stuffed 20 inmates into cells that normally housed 6. Haci and his brother were both arrested; they shared a prison bed, taking turns sleeping.

In the summer of 2013, as the Öcalan-Erdoğan peace process strengthened hopes of a solution to the Kurdish dispute, Haci was released after three years in prison. "I came out six months later," Birlik recalled. "Haci went back to working with the trade unions." A year later, ISIS attacked the Yazidis, a minority group with Kurdish ties, in the Sinjar region in northeast Iraq, close to Kobanî and Turkey's Syria border. Yazidi men were massacred and their women were turned into sex slaves. Kurdish fighters from the Rojava canton in Syria battled ISIS and opened a safe passage for the Yazidis; tens of thousands of Yazidis crossed the border and found refuge in the Kurdish cities and towns in southeastern Turkey. As desperate Yazidis arrived in Şırnak,

138 Kurdish activists, including Haci, reached out and helped them set up a camp.

The end of the peace process in the summer of 2015 turned Haci and many other young Kurds into armed rebels, as they began setting up barricades in the neighborhood of Dicle to defend the community from the Turkish military. On the evening of October 3, Birlik was home waiting for his wife Leila, a member of the Turkish Parliament who had been elected as the HDP candidate from Şırnak.

A gun battle was raging in another neighborhood between the Kurds and the military. Leila had gone there to try to help the civilians and monitor the situation when she received a phone call informing her that someone had been killed in Dicle, where there had been fighing. "A policeman tagged her on Twitter and said, 'We killed your brother-in-law," Birlik recalled. "'Come get his body.'" The police had tossed Haci's body outside the hospital and kicked it around in the open. "He had two long range bullets in his legs and 26 short range bullets in his face and chest," Birlik recalled. "He was 28 years old and they had shot him 28 times." Birlik never found out how his brother died.

The war in the southeast got worse after I left. Between the winter of 2015 and the summer of 2016, Erdoğan's military operations against the Kurds killed hundreds and destroyed tens of thousands of homes. Sur was rubble. Nuseybin was rubble. Cizre was rubble. Mardin was rubble. Every Kurdish town seemed to have been turned into Silvan.

The young Kurdish rebels who had manned the barricades
in Silvan were either killed or pushed into the mountains of
Qandil in Iraq. The International Crisis Group estimated that
519 Kurdish fighters, 517 security personnel, and at least 271
civilians were killed between July 2015 and June 2016. About
200 others couldn't be identified. Turkish air force jets continued bombing PKK camps in the Iraqi mountains; no reliable
numbers of the deaths there were available. "The trenches they
dug have become their graves and the bombs they planted to
divide the nation have exploded in their own hands," Erdoğan
said at a meeting with the families of soldiers killed in battle.

Erdoğan's war is winning the PKK recruits as bleak tales of
war crimes spread among the Kurdish populations. If the Kurds
had sung ballads of the valiant battle to save Kobanî from ISIS,
a new generation is growing up to elegies for Cizre, a town of
100,000 people, about four hours from Diyarbakır, where more
than a hundred people who had sought shelter in basements
were killed. "The buildings were shattered by artillery, tank fire
and street fighting, according to local people," Jeremy Bowen,
a correspondent with the BBC, reported. "When the curfew
ended and the fighting stopped, Turkish security forces sent in
bulldozers to level the ruins."

Turkey's Kurds speak of Cizre with horror, and many
believe that the Turkish army had burned the people in the
basements alive. No independent investigations were carried
out. I was told that the Kurdish youngsters fighting behind the
barricades were mostly born during the Turkish military campaigns of the 1990s. Kurds call them "the children of storm."

140   There is increasing worry that stories of Erdoğan's war against the Kurds will create another militant generation.

The war has boomeranged from the Kurdish periphery to the Turkish center. In February 2016, Kurdistan Freedom Falcons, a radical splinter group of the PKK, bombed a convoy of buses in Ankara and killed 28 military personnel and 2 civilians. A month later, a car bomb near the prime minister's office in Ankara killed 37 people. In June, the Kurdistan Freedom Falcons attacked another bus carrying policemen in central Istanbul and killed 12 people. Turkish television broadcast long funerals of the soldiers killed in battle.

Nationalist feelings and hostility toward Kurds have intensified, yet a few journalists, activists, and academics have spoken out against the military operations in the southeast. Academics for Peace, a group of Turkish scholars and teachers from across the country, lent their names to a petition titled, "We Will Not be a Party to This Crime." Around 1,100 academics from 90 Turkish universities and 355 academics from other countries signed the petition. They spoke out against the sieges of Kurdish towns, the denial of basic amenities to besieged citizens, and they bemoaned the use of weapons associated with wartime. "We, as academics and researchers working on and/or in Turkey, declare that we will not be a party to this massacre by remaining silent and demand an immediate end to the violence perpetrated by the state," the professors declared. They called upon the Turkish government to grant independent observers access to the areas of conflict and to return to peace negotiations.

The next day President Erdoğan harangued them in a televised speech. "Hey, you so-called intellectuals!" Erdoğan said.

"You are nothing like intellectuals. You are ignorant and dark, not even knowing about the east or the southeast." Sedat Peker, the mob boss imprisoned during the Ergenekon trials who had repositioned himself as a supporter of the AKP since his release, posted a threat on his personal website. "We will spill our blood, and we will take a shower in your blood," Peker wrote.

Several academics were arrested. A campaign smearing them as supporters of terrorists ran in pro-government newspapers. One newspaper printed photographs and names of hundreds of the signatories. Across Turkey, university authorities started disciplinary proceedings against the signatories. Police began searching houses. Crosses were painted on the doors of certain professors at a university in Ankara.

Having vanquished the military establishment, the Gülenist press, the Kurdish insurgents, and the intellectual elite, Erdoğan set his sights on Selahattin Demirtaş and the politicians of the HDP, who had so humiliated him in the June 2015 elections. In May 2016, Erdoğan pushed through a bill to stop granting members of Parliament immunity from prosecution, which would allow HDP lawmakers to face charges under Turkey's broad and vague anti-terror laws.

If members of the HDP were convicted, fresh elections would be held for their parliamentary seats. The political climate of intense nationalism, oppositional disarray, and Erdoğan's supremacy over all Turkish institutions is likely to ensure landslide victories for the AKP. The electoral support for constitutional changes for the executive presidency that Demirtaş denied Erdoğan last year seems close to the strongman's grasp.

On a recent summer morning, Demirtaş, who has been dealing with one of the most volatile periods of his political career, was flying out of Turkey on a work trip. He agreed to meet me at an airport lounge reserved for the Turkish government elite. Demirtaş was working on his iPad in a corner of the plush waiting lounge. A small man with a prominent nose and a boyish smile, Demirtaş was at ease in a light linen jacket and blue trousers. He transformed as he spoke about the military operations in the southeast; suppressed anger bubbled under his words. "The Turkish state is not fighting the PKK, it is fighting the Kurds," Demirtaş said, his voice calm and deliberate. "The military operations are against the Kurdish people. They want to decimate Kurdish politics, they want to eliminate Kurds as a collective, turn us into obedient subjects."

Since the end of the peace process and the eruption of all-out war, Demirtaş and his colleagues had spent most of their time in the southeast seeking to stand by their people. They had little material influence but they had spoken out against the operations and sought an end to violence. "When I went to Cizre, it was an occupied city, a city completely destroyed. The state had shown its most inhuman face," he said.

Demirtaş sees the latest insurgency as part of a long war between the Kurds seeking their own future and the Turkish republic trying to subdue and transform them into submissive citizens. He feels the Kurds have been lonely and powerless ever since Atatürk founded the Turkish republic in 1923, but he draws strength from the political successes of the Kurds in northern Iraq and Syria, where they have established de facto autonomous regions and earned the support of the United

States. "We are not alone," he said, although his words seemed
to be aimed at convincing himself.

The revocation of immunity posed a serious danger to Demirtaş and his colleagues, as they face likely prosecution and banishment from Parliament. "A judge can easily find a reason to send us to prison," Demirtaş said. He had decided to challenge the revocation law in higher courts, and he seemed strangely hopeful. "A totalitarian leader without a mask is easier to fight," Demirtaş told me. "He won't determine the future of Turkey." I wasn't so sure.

Conclusion

A vocabulary of despair has come to dominate our world. Majoritarian politics. Populism. Militant nationalism. Xenophobia. Strongmen. Authoritarianism. In various permutations, these words and concepts are increasingly used to describe the current moment. The neoliberal ideas of the early nineties imagining the world remaking itself by imitating the Western model of liberal democracy and globalized capitalism didn't quite work out.

The intensified, ever-visible, video-recorded killings of African-American men by American law enforcement officers have eroded the global perception of the United States as an exemplar of liberal democracy and citizenship equality. The rise of Donald Trump and his racist, xenophobic rhetoric has further affected America's ability to wield moral influence and speak about liberal democratic traditions abroad. The election year has also seen a rise of hate crimes against American Muslims—a 78 percent increase in 2015, according to a report by California State University's Center for the Study of Hate and Extremism—which is hurting America's great success story of integrating immigrants of all races and creeds. An era of anxiety about liberalism in America and American behavior in the world dawned with the election of Donald Trump. David Remnick, the editor of *The New Yorker*, precisely described it as "a triumph for the forces, at home and abroad, of nativism, authoritarianism, misogyny, and racism" and "a sickening event in the history of the United States and liberal democracy."

The weeks following the referendum on Britain's exit from the European Union saw the rise of attacks on immigrants, along with a decrease in the value of the pound and hikes in food prices. According to the London Mayor's office, 2,300 racial and hate crimes were recorded in the month and a half after the Brexit vote. Many recall Theresa May's "go home" billboard vans in 2013, which the then-Home Secretary dispatched through immigrant neighborhoods in London urging illegal immigrants to "go home or face arrest." Theresa May is now the Prime Minister of Great Britain.

The Syrian refugee crisis has unleashed a lot of anxiety in Europe about demographic and cultural changes and the eroding of social benefits. Many fear that Europe "is sleepwalking its way back to the 1930s," in the words of Ivan Krastev, chairman of the Centre for Liberal Strategies in Bulgaria. Jaroslaw Kaczynski, the Premier of Poland, has argued that refugees would bring disease into Poland.

146   Hungarian Prime Minister Victor Orbán has refused to accept any refugees in a EU-led distribution process and has spoken about the threat to Europe's "Christian values" from the refugees. Orbán also energetically built a barbed-wire fence along Hungary's borders with Croatia and Serbia to keep the refugees out and arrested tens of thousands who crossed into his country. However, he wasn't the first to build a fence; Greece had built one on its land border with Turkey in 2012. After the land routes were closed, refugees resorted to perilous journeys toward Europe by sea. Austria, Slovenia, Macedonia, and Bulgaria built their own barbed-wire fences. In October 2016, the French evacuated and shut down a massive refugee camp in Calais. Since the fall of the Berlin Wall, European countries have built or started 750 miles of anti-immigrant fencing at a cost of at least $570 million.

Another dramatic result of the Syrian refugee crisis was a change in the balance of power between the European Union and Turkey. Turkey has hosted more than three million Syrian refugees—more than any other nation. Turkey also served as a place of rest and transit for hundreds of thousands more, who were willing to risk their lives across turbulent seas to make it to Europe. The presence of millions of refugees in his domain, a short boat ride from European shores, turned Erdoğan into the gatekeeper of Europe. The leverage that the refugee crisis gave Erdoğan has muted criticism of his authoritarian behavior. A European Union report on the abysmal state of democracy in Turkey was supposed to have been released before the November 2015 elections, but it was delayed.

In March 2016, the European Union signed a deal to seek the help of Turkey in controlling the flow of refugees into its borders. The Turks agreed to take back those who snuck into EU territory illegally, and for each of the repatriated, Europe would legally settle one Syrian refugee from a camp in Turkey. Those who fled from Afghanistan, Iraq, and Africa were left out, but the EU promised $6.6 billion in aid to Turkey to help it deal with the refugees it hosted. The EU also promised visa-free travel for Turkish citizens if the country agreed to bring its broad anti-terror laws within EU standards, which could have been Erdoğan's most enduring gift to his countrymen, who have millions of kin living and working across Europe. The number of refugee arrivals on Greek shores reduced considerably in the months after the deal, but Turkish reluctance to modify its laws turned out to be surprisingly intense, and relations with the EU turned bitter. As the future of the refugee deal turned glum, Turkey itself faced its largest political crisis on July 15, 2016.

About nine on the evening of July 15, Turkish soldiers commandeering tanks and armored vehicles blocked and seized the Bosphorus Bridge connecting the Asian and European parts of Istanbul. A faction of the Turkish Army officers had started a coup against the Erdoğan government. Renegade soldiers arrested General Hulusi Akar, the Army's Chief of General Staff, and held him along with several other senior military officers at an airbase. Among Akar's kidnappers was his private secretary, Major General Mehmet Dişli, who later confessed to have been a follower of Gülen for more than 30 years. The *Hurriyet* newspaper reported that Dişli and other coup plotters tried to force Akar to sign and read to the public a declaration in support of the coup, holding him at gunpoint and tying a belt around his neck when he refused. After his rescue, Akar claimed that his kidnappers had offered to put him in touch with their "opinion leader, Gülen."

Renegade officers had ordered their followers across Turkey to block main roads and take over airports and major institutions of government. Tanks appeared on the streets of Ankara. F-16 fighter jets flown by pilots loyal to the putschists took to the skies. "Fighters planes were flying very low. They made such terrifying noise. Our windows were rattling. We hid in a corner of the apartment and hoped it will pass," Sara Nasser, a young American living in Istanbul, told me. Turkish lawmakers were at work inside the parliament building in Ankara when jets commandeered by rebels dropped bombs on it. Parts of the parliament were reduced to rubble; several people were injured. Lawmakers from all four political parties—Erdoğan's AKP, the Kemalist CHP, the ultranationalist MHP, the pro-Kurdish HDP—came together and spoke out against the coup attempt. Outside, on the streets of Ankara, insurgent helicopters opened fire on police officers and civilians opposing the coup.

Erdoğan was on holiday in Marmaris, an Aegean Sea resort town. Coup plotters sent a helicopter-borne team of soldiers to capture, and perhaps, kill him. They got into a gun battle with Erdoğan's guards, and he escaped unhurt. Overcoming the initial shock, Turkish citizens came out onto the streets to protest the coup attempt and battle rebel soldiers. A putschist sniper shot at civilians from a post of the Bosphorus Bridge. Turkey

had military coups in 1960, 1971, 1980, and 1997, but never
before had Turkish soldiers opened fire on Turkish civilians.

A convoy of army trucks surrounded the headquarters of
the Turkish Radio and Television Corporation, and announced
their takeover and the imposition of martial law on the state
broadcaster. About half past midnight, Erdoğan managed to use
Facetime on his iPhone to call a presenter on CNN Turk, who
took his video call and held out her phone toward the rolling
cameras, helping the besieged President address the Turkish
nation. Erdoğan urged the people of Turkey to gather against
the coup on public squares and airports. "There is no power
higher than the power of the people," he said.

Turks, including those who have been critical of Erdoğan's
authoritarian ways, came out in immense numbers against the
coup, and most of the military leaders and soldiers stayed loyal
to the government. The First Army's General Ümit Dündar
marshaled his troops and took control of Ataturk Airport,
allowing Erdoğan to finally land in Istanbul late in the night
of the coup. Thousands welcomed him. He blamed the coup
on "Pennsylvania," his preferred nickname for Gülen. "This is
an act of treason and they will pay heavily," Erdoğan told the
gathering.

By the morning of July 16, it was evident that the coup had
failed. Civilians danced on abandoned tanks left by the soldiers on the Bosphorus Bridge. "Years later, when I remember
that night, I'll remember everyone's faces glowing with concern
in the cold, pale light of their phone screens as they walked as
fast as their legs would allow," wrote Busra Erkara, a Turkish
journalist. More than 230 people, including 145 civilians who

150   confronted the putschists, were killed. More than two thousands were injured.

A majority of Turks, who were traumatized by the brutality of the coup attempt, rallied around Erdoğan, whom they
saw narrowly escape from being toppled and killed. Erdoğan
dropped about two thousand lawsuits against Turkish citizens
who he had charged with insulting him. He held rallies of unity
with the opposition leaders of the CHP and the MHP, overcoming the traditional secular versus religious divide. (He left out
the Kurds, though they also came out against the coup.) Even
his most fierce critics in the secular press stood behind him.
For more than a month after the coup, Erdoğan's government
organized gatherings known as "Democracy Watches" at public
squares throughout the country.

One August evening I watched several thousand men
and women at one such gathering at Taksim Square and Gezi
Park. Buildings by the square were covered in enormous red
Turkish flags and posters denouncing the failed coup. Faces of
men and women killed by renegade soldiers were plastered on
the walls of the Taksim Square subway station, their names,
the place and date of their murder written below. A massive
stage was erected close to Gezi Park; a giant projector on the
stage played scenes from the night of the coup, showcasing
the brutality of the coup plotters, the courage of the people
opposing them, and, above all, the face and voice of President
Recep Tayyip Erdoğan. The crowd waved and sang. The lyrics
of a frequently played song, accompanied by catchy militaris-
tic beats, seemed to simply be three words sung over and over
again: *Recep. Tayyip. Erdoğan.*

The cult of Erdoğan was more powerful than ever, and his revenge was pitiless. Turkey was descending into chaos, tolerance for any criticism of the President was at its lowest, and its relationship with the Europeans and the Americans was fraught. The United States and the European Union had spoken out against the coup (not strongly enough, from Turkish perspective) but also advised Erdoğan to follow the rule of law and not use the failed coup as an excuse to abuse his authority. Several European countries were slow in coming out against the coup. The muted Western reaction riled up the Turks; conspiracy theories surfaced in the Turkish public sphere that the West might have been happy to see the coup succeed. "Not a single person has come to give condolences either from the European Union ... or from the West," Erdoğan told his supporters in a speech weeks after the coup. "And then they say that 'Erdoğan has got so angry'! Those countries or leaders who are not worried about Turkey's democracy, the lives of our people, its future—while being so worried about the fate of the putschists—cannot be our friends."

Turkey demanded the U.S. extradite Gülen to be tried in Turkey for the failed coup attempt. Americans sought credible proof and emphasized following due process. Turkey hasn't been able to provide exact, actionable evidence—something that rarely exists in such cases. A spike in anti-Americanism followed as pro-Erdoğan Turks saw the U.S. as protecting Gülen. Talk about Gülen's relationship with the Central Intelligence Agency began circulating. His permanent residence granted through the "Alien of Extraordinary Ability" program had succeeded only when a former CIA official and a former U.S.

152   Ambassador to Turkey wrote letters in his support. A former
        head of the Turkish intelligence claimed in his memoirs that
        American intelligence operatives relied on the Gülenist school
        network in Central Asia and Africa for support, at times pre-
        tending to be English teachers in Gülenist academies.

        The ambivalence of the American and European response
        to the coup made Erdoğan even angrier, who mounted an
        unprecedented purge of suspected Gülenists and coup-sup-
        porters from all kinds of Turkish institutions. Between July and
        November, more than a 100,000 people were sacked from the
        military, police, judiciary, university, and other sectors. About
        40,000 were arrested, and to make room for increasing wave
        of detainees, Turkey even released a large number of criminals
        from its prisons. Ibrahim Kalin, the spokesperson for Erdoğan,
        compared the purges to "the *Einigungsvertrag* process, in which
        about half a million East German state employees were sacked
        or suspended during the German reunification over their links
        to the old regime."

        The evidence in most cases is thin: a person's record of
        having attended a Gülenist school has been enough to get him
        arrested. The Turkish press reported that most people under
        investigation were using *ByLock*, an instant messaging service,
        which Turkey's National Intelligence Organization claims was
        developed and used by Gülenists. The flaws in the investigations
        are massive. "For example, someone has lost their job because
        they shared the same ADSL in a building with neighbors who
        included suspected Gülenists," wrote Murat Atkin, the editor of
        Hurriyet Daily News. "There are other complaints about some-
        one losing their job because they once took out housing credit

from Bank Asya"—a Gülenist bank—"because a construction
company had an agreement with them."

The arrests and purges initially targeted journalists who worked for or published in the Gülen media, but were soon expanded to target a wide range of critics and political opponents. More than 100 journalists have been detained in Turkey after the coup, according to the Committee to Protect Journalists. Scores of media outlets have been closed. Press credentials of more than 300 journalists have been cancelled. Among the arrested were some of the best-known names in the Turkish press—pro-Gülen columnists Şahin Alpay and Nazlı Ilıcak, who are in their seventies; prominent liberal novelists Aslı Erdoğan and Ahmet Altan; Ahmet's brother Mehmet Altan, a writer and professor of economics at an Istanbul university. The Altan brothers were charged with "giving subliminal messages to rally coup supporters on a television show" that was broadcast the night before the coup.

Erdoğan's wrath expanded from arresting Gulenists to targeting the Kurds as well. Erol Önderoğlu, who represented Reporters Without Borders in Turkey, Şebnem Korur Fincancı, who headed the Human Rights Foundation of Turkey, Ahmet Nesin, a writer, and İnan Kızılkaya, the editor of the now-shuttered Kurdish newspaper *Özgür Gündem*, were all arrested and charged with carrying out "terrorist propaganda" for the PKK. Nadire Mater, the editor of left-leaning website Bianet, who worked as the editor of *Özgür Gündem* for a day as a show of solidarity, were also put on trial. Önderoğlu and Fincancı spent about four months in prison before being released by an Istanbul court in November. Officials raided and closed IMC TV,

154   a pro-Kurdish television network. Several others newspapers
that focused on the Kurdish question were shut down and their
journalists arrested.

Erdoğan also turned to the Kemalist elite. *Cumhuriyet*, one
of the oldest and most respected opposition papers of the country and long a critic of both Erdoğan and Gülen, was raided, and
its editor and twelve others colleagues were arrested. The absurd
charge against them was that they published stories supporting
Kurdish rebels and legitimizing the coup—before it happened.

After the coup the Kurds had reached out to Erdoğan with
an offer of peace, but he was in no mood to mend fences. "Some
of their leaders reached out to (former president) Abdullah Gül
and sought his help in mediating with Erdoğan. Kurds don't like
the military or the Gulenists and wanted to make peace," a senior
AKP member told me. Erdoğan was unforgiving. Hostilities
with the PKK resurfaced. Erdoğan removed more than 1,100
teachers from their jobs for suspected links with the PKK. Most
of them had signed petitions against the military operations of
2015, calling for peace in the Turkish southeast.

Soon after that, Turkish police arrested the co-mayors
of Diyarbakır and followed it up by arresting the senior-most
leaders of the pro-Kurdish party. Selahattin Demirtaş and Figen
Yüksekdağ, the co-chairs of the People's Democratic Party, were
detained in late October. Ten other Kurdish parliamentarians
were imprisoned. The arrests of Kurdish politicians amount to
physically removing them from the political arena and erasing
their certain opposition to the unfinished business of Erdoğan's
executive presidency, including a referendum to transform the
parliamentary system into a presidential one, which would grant

him even greater powers. Few internal or external checks remain
on Erdoğan's path to greater power and control over Turkey. He
has laughed off the criticisms of a struggling European Union,
and a Trump presidency is soothing news for strongmen.
"Freedom of thought no longer exists," novelist Orhan Pamuk
lamented in a recent essay. "We are distancing ourselves at high
speed from a state of law and heading towards a regime of terror."

On the night of the coup in Turkey, I was already in a city experi-
encing a regime of terror. Not in Erdoğan's Turkey, but in Modi's
world. I was in Srinagar, the biggest city in Indian-controlled-
Kashmir, with my parents. A week before the coup attempt in
Turkey, on July 8, Burhan Wani, a 22-year-old rebel, was shot
dead by Indian soldiers and police officers in a small village.
News of his killing spread as fast as the bullets that had hit him.
Cellphones, emails, and social media went wild: "They've killed
Burhan! They've killed Burhan!" Everybody called Burhan by his
first name.

He had become an Internet sensation over the past year,
first in Kashmir, then in India and Pakistan, after putting
together a small band of Kashmiri militants. Barely out of their
teens, they had taken to the forest and social media to challenge
the Indian government. Photos they posted on Facebook show
them in military fatigues and with stubbly chins, posing with
AK-47s against backdrops of apple orchards or mountains. In
one video, Burhan plays cricket.

There is no record of Burhan and his crew waging any attack.
Their rebellion was symbolic, a war of images against India's
continuing occupation of Kashmir, where about half a million

156   of its soldiers, paramilitary, and armed police are still stationed.

According to top police officials, Burhan and two other militants were killed on the evening of July 8 in a gun battle that broke out after Indian soldiers and Kashmiri police surrounded the house in which they had sought shelter. Protests erupted on the day of Burhan's funeral and were repressed by Indian troops with indiscriminate force, including pellet guns. About fifty people had been killed and 3,100 injured, nearly half of them Indian troops, but also children as young as four. Instead of opening political negotiations to address Kashmiris' calls for independence, India continues to unabashedly use military force to maintain a status quo that for years has suffocated millions in the region.

When I first saw the photos of Burhan and his boys, I thought: another generation of young Kashmiris about to be consumed. Those apple orchards and mountains in the background, which I know intimately and call home, brought back memories of the early 1990s, when I was a teenager in southern Kashmir. An armed insurgency supported by Pakistan and a popular rebellion were both underway then, triggered by the Indian government's meddling in a recent state election.

By the time the insurgency was quashed in the late 2000s, more than 70,000 militants, soldiers, and civilians had been killed. Still, hundreds of thousands of Kashmiris would occasionally take to the streets. Indian troops continued to respond with violence, even against civilians armed with nothing or nothing more than stones. Hardly any soldier has been prosecuted for civilian killings because Indian law has long granted immunity to troops posted in Kashmir and other troubled regions. (A recent decision by India's Supreme Court may change this.)

Burhan came of age with this inheritance of loss and rage. He was 15, a top-ranking student from a middle-class family, in 2010—that summer alone Indian forces killed more than 110 Kashmiri protesters. One afternoon that year, Indian police officers posted in Burhan's town reportedly sent him and his brother Khalid to fetch cigarettes, and then beat up the boys when they returned. Humiliated, Burhan left for the mountains and joined a tiny group of militants. Then last year, Khalid, who was doing post-graduate work in economics, was killed by Indian soldiers.

On the morning of July 9, Burhan's body was brought to a vast open ground in Tral, his hometown, about twenty-five miles east of Srinagar. In the early hours, the photojournalist Javed Dar saw that hundreds of people who had come from nearby villages were sleeping on the streets, some using rocks as pillows. About 200,000 people are reported to have attended the funeral throughout the day. Prayers were repeated several times to accommodate newcomers.

As Kashmiris seethed with desperate anger that day, Indian paramilitaries and police were deployed across the region. In hundreds of locations, people came out to mourn Burhan and raise their voices against the Indian occupation. The vast majority were unarmed. In some places, protesters picked up stones and charged at camps of Indian soldiers and police. The troops responded with a brutality rare even by the grim standards of their record in Kashmir. They fired bullets, tear gas, and lead pellets. Soon, the Indian government imposed a military curfew.

I reached Kashmir from Delhi on July 11, and the next morning when I woke up in my parents' house in southern Srinagar,
I heard only crickets chirping in the backyard. The streets were
desolate except for groups of Indian paramilitary troops with
guns and bamboo sticks. The pro-India politicians who run the
Kashmir government had all but disappeared from public view.
Kashmiris, as they do in crisis, turned to themselves for support. At Shri Maharaja Hari Singh Hospital in central Srinagar,
where the injured had been brought by the hundreds, scores of
volunteers were offering medicine, money, clothes and care to
the patients and their families.

I walked into an ophthalmology ward. There were about
twenty beds with a teenager or young man in each, their relatives standing around in anxious huddles. Almost every patient
had large, black sunglasses. "Seventy-two patients with pellet injuries arrived here in one day," one doctor told me. SMHS
Hospital alone had received more than 180 people with serious
wounds to the eyes. A single shot from a pellet gun sprays more
than a hundred pellets. A pellet is a high-velocity projectile two
millimeter to four millimeter around and with sharp edges. It
doesn't simply penetrate an eye; it ricochets inside it, tearing
the retina and the optic nerves, scooping out flesh and bone.

I walked through the hospital with Dr. Javed Shafi, a surgeon in his early fourties, as he was making bed calls with his
patients.

The day before he had operated on Shafia Jan, a pale, slim
woman in her mid-twenties from Arwani, a village about fifty
miles south. She had stepped out of her house after hearing
commotion on the street during protests following Burhan's

death, she explained. A police officer fired his pump-action gun toward her. "I didn't feel anything at first. Then, my left leg crumbled and I fell. I saw my intestines falling out," Shafia told me. She pushed her guts back into the wound and held them in with her hands. Scores of pellets had pierced her lower abdomen, opening up the scars of an earlier C-section.

Omar Nazir, a reed-thin boy of twelve, barely filled one corner of his bed. A thick swathe of bandages formed a cross across his chest and belly. He had black, adult-size glasses. "He's lost both his eyes," Shafi said. Doctors had yet to deliver the news to Nazir Ahmad, the boy's father, a day laborer in Pulwama, a district in southern Kashmir, but he already seemed to know. Ahmad, tall and wiry, looked at the doctor, his eyes liquid with entreaty: "Dr. Sahib, we own one-fifth of an acre of land in the village. I will sell all my land, but please make him see."

In other corners of the hospital: A young man with the face of Adrian Brody whose penis had to be amputated because it had been shredded by pellets. A four-year-old girl, her legs and abdomen riddled by what she called "firecrackers." And Insha Malik. I had read about fourteen-year-old Insha in that morning's paper. The photograph accompanying the article showed a face with red wart-like wounds. Her nasal bridge was a lump of raw flesh held together by black surgical thread. The bloodied lids of her left eye had been sown shut. Her right eye was a red alloy of blood, flesh, bone and metal.

Insha was in the surgical intensive care unit of SMHS Hospital, a few rooms away from the ward I visited with Shafi. Afroza Malik, her mother, a woman in her early fifties, sat right by the Intensive Care Unit door on the bare floor. Her husband,

160 who had a leg injury from an earlier accident, was lying on a blanket, his head in his wife's lap. She was stroking his graying hair. Afroza explained that on July 12, she, Insha, and several relatives had taken refuge in an upstairs room of their two-story house in Sedew, a tiny village forty miles south of Srinagar. They closed the thick wooden windows and sat on the floor. They heard gunshots and tear gas canisters being fired. A loud noise followed. A pellet gun had been fired at the window. Insha was sitting nearby. "The window was blown to pieces," Afroza told me. "I heard her wail and saw blood flowing out of her eyes. She fell on the floor."

A few days later, the police raided the offices of *Greater Kashmir*, the daily that had run that story about Insha, as well as several other local newspapers, and shut down the printing presses. A few weeks later, *Kashmir Reader*, another English-language newspaper, was banned and shut down by the government. The authorities' familiar silencing routine had begun again. Indian officials and thought leaders fell back on tired rituals of obfuscation and denial. Between July and November, more than 90 people were killed, with some 17,000 injured. Doctors at hospitals in Kashmir estimated that about 1,100 young men and teenagers have been hit in their eyes and lost their vision to varying degrees. The entire population of the Valley of Kashmir was put under de-facto imprisonment with a four month long military curfew.

After a mid-September attack by Pakistani militants killed 19 Indian soldiers in a camp near the northern Kashmir town of Uri, a new season of nationalist fury erupted across India.

Modi's strongman image was at stake and he promised revenge.
Right-wing television anchors bayed for Pakistani blood and
action against "traitors" who harbored critical thoughts. An
English language television network refurbished its newsroom
as a war room, and a lead anchor appeared on the show wearing fatigues. A well-known defense analyst for the right-wing
Times Now network argued it was time to use nuclear weapons against Pakistan: an Indian nuclear attack could wipe out
Pakistan completely; a Pakistani retaliation could kill 500 million Indians, but it would still leave half of India alive, with the
chance to rise again as a great nation unencumbered by the
presence of Pakistan. A few weeks later, Indian troops attacked
Pakistani position across the Line of Control, claiming that
"surgical strikes" by Indian forces in Pakistan-controlled-
Kashmir had caused serious damage to the terrorist camps.
Pakistan brushed it aside as the usual exchange of fire that
intermittently takes place across the Line of Control. India film
producers banned Pakistani actors from working in their movies. Pakistani authorities banned the release of Indian movies in
the country.

The air in New Delhi has remained thick with xenophobia,
suspicion, and fear. Modi's pictures with soldiers celebrating
the "surgical strikes" have appeared across the country. The
whipping up of jingoism is linked to forthcoming elections in
Uttar Pradesh, the largest Indian state, where the BJP is stak-
ing a claim to power. Several opposition politicians have been
arrested. Police attacked protests against the disappearance
of Mohammad Najeeb, a biotechnology student at Jawaharlal

162   Nehru University in New Delhi. Najeeb was assaulted by activ-
        ists from ABVP, the student wing of the RSS, in October, and
        went missing afterwards. A dubious murder charge was filed
        against Nandini Sundar, a leading sociologist at the Delhi School
        of Economics, whose research and writing have revealed abuse
        of state power in Chattisgarh, a central Indian state wracked
        by the battle between Maoist rebels and Indian troops. A lead-
        ing liberal television network, New Delhi Television India, was
        ordered to go off air for a day for "incorrect" reporting of a terror-
        ist attack. A national outcry eventually made the Modi regime
        revert the decision. "Nationalism is used to stifle all thinking,"
        wrote Pratap Bhanu Mehta, one of India's foremost public intel-
        lectuals. "The cultivation of collective narcissism to stifle all
        individuality, the promulgation of uncontested definitions of
        nationalism to pre-empt all debate over genuine national inter-
        est, the constant hunt for contrived enemies of the nation, is
        suffocating thought."

            On most mornings it takes an act of will to read the news-
        papers in Modi's India. Yet Prime Minister Modi's chosen
        cabinet colleagues do display great acts of empathy and love. In
        early October, Ravin Sisodia, who was among the several men
        arrested for the lynching of Mohammad Akhlaq in Dadri vil-
        lage outside New Delhi, died of kidney failure in prison at the
        age of 22. The villagers draped his body in India's national flag
        and honored him as a martyr. Hate speeches calling for uproot-
        ing and killing Muslims were made. Among the men who joined
        the funeral were several prominent members of Modi's party
        and Mahesh Sharma, Modi's culture minister. Sharma tweeted

photographs of himself in a white *kurta* pajama, hands folded,
head bent, offering his respects at the funeral of a man who was
jailed for lynching and murder. The age of majoritarian politics
was here to stay, and all Modi had to do was stay silent.

PART ONE:

Pratap Bhanu Mehta's *The Burden of Democracy* is a necessary book
about the challenges and opportunities of democracy in India. Pankaj
Mishra's *Temptations of the West* is a brilliant survey of India after the
great transformation of the early nineties, which saw the rise of religious
politics and economic liberalization. Suketu Mehta's *Maximum City:
Bombay Lost and Found* has some of the most searing accounts of religious
politics and violence in India. Thomas Blom Hanson's *The Saffron Wave* is a
necessary read on the rise of Hindu nationalism in modern India. Nilanjan
Mukhopadhyay's *Narendra Modi: The Man, The Times* is an important
biographical study of Modi and his rise. Manoj Mitta's *The Fiction of
Fact-Finding* is one of the most valuable investigations in the allegations
of Modi's complicity in the 2002 Gujarat violence and subsequent official
investigations. Mukul Kesavan's *Secular Common Sense* is one of the most
rewarding analyses of Indian secularism. The essays and multiple books of
the political psychologist Ashis Nandy are required reading on modern India.

PART TWO:

Kerem Oktem's *Angry Nation: Turkey Since 1989* is a brilliant account
of the transformation of Turkey in the past two decades. Jenny White's
Muslim Nationalism and the New Turks is one of the most persuasive
anthropological accounts of Erdoğan's Turkey. Joshua D Hendrick's *Gülen:
The Ambiguous Politics of Market Islam in Turkey and the World* is the one of
the best studies of the Gülen movement. Nilüfer Göle's *Islam in Europe: The
Lure of Fundamentalism and the Allure of Cosmopolitanism* and *The Forbidden
Modern: Civilization and Veiling* are necessary reading on understanding
the place of religion in public sphere in Turkey. Andrew Mango's *Ataturk*
is the most readable biography of the founder of the Turkish republic.
Mustafa Akyol's *Islam without Extremes* is an important account of the
early years of the AKP and an exploration of Islam and democracy. Orhan
Pamuk's *A Strangeness in My Mind* is a great novel in the tradition of
Stendhal's *The Red and The Black*, but also the best social history of modern
Istanbul. Christopher de Bellaigue's *Rebel Land: Among Turkey's Forgotten
People* is necessary reading on Kurdish and Armenian questions and their
relationship with mainland Turkey. The movies of Nuri Bilge Ceylan and
Yesim Ustuaoglu must be watched to understand the soul of modern
Turkey.

NOTES

14 "one in which the executive branch": http://www.journalofdemocracy.org/article/authoritarian-resurgence-autocratic-legalism-venezuela

19 left thousands dead: https://sabrangindia.in/in-fact/yatra-lk-advani

19 earned Advani's confidence: L. K. Advani, *My Country, My Life*, Rupa Publications, 2008.

20 paraded through Ahmedabad: http://www.nytimes.com/interactive/2014/04/06/world/asia/modi-gujarat-riots-timeline.html

20 complicit in the carnage: https://www.hrw.org/reports/2002/india/

20 "child-producing centers": http://www.outlookindia.com/website/story/should-we-run-relief-camps-open-child-producing-centres/217398

21 no access to basic amenities: http://www.nytimes.com/2014/04/19/opinion/being-muslim-under-narendra-modi.html

22 mill owners began investing: http://indiatoday.intoday.in/story/recession-in-gujarat-textile-industry-reaches-crisis-proportions/1/360543.html

24 Modi had won over: http://www.thehinducentre.com/verdict/commentary/article5848327.ece

29 as many as 450,000 people: http://www.livemint.com/Politics/hLaMOzbcWwlS8fEzxFvFNI/Resurrecting-Brand-Hyderabad.html

31 "We worship Lord Ganesha": https://www.theguardian.com/world/2014/oct/28/indian-prime-minister-genetic-science-existed-ancient-times

33 Modi's majoritarianism: http://india.blogs.nytimes.com/2013/06/16/bihar-ally-nitish-kumar-leaves-opposition-coalition-over-modis-elevation/

34 "I will fight such an idea": Sankarshan Thakur, *Single Man: Life and Times of Nitish Kumar of Bihar,* Harper Collins India, 2014

35 "Those who intend to stop Narendra Modi": http://indianexpress.com/article/india/politics/bjp-nominee-to-modi-critics-you-will-soon-be-in-pak-not-india/

35 "Mother Ganges has called me": http://timesofindia.indiatimes.com/news/Narendra-Modi-files-nomination-says-Ma-Ganga-has-called-me-to-Varanasi/articleshow/34147322.cms

36 814 million Indians voted: http://blogs.reuters.com/

india/2014/04/03/facts-and-figures-for-the-2014-general-election/

38 **according to police officials:** http://www.caravanmagazine.in/reportage/separation

38 **"save the honor of daughters and daughters-in-law":** http://www.ndtv.com/elections-news/governments-pink-revolution-destroying-cattle-says-narendra-modi-555981

40 **"Beggars have turned millionaires":** http://scroll.in/article/660535/this-election-is-a-fight-for-honour-and-revenge-amit-shah-tells-jat-audience-in-riot-areas

44 **"the welfare of mother India":** http://indianexpress.com/article/india/india-others/full-text-prime-minister-narendra-modis-speech-on-68th-independence-day/#sthash.VlIES9hC.dpuf

45 **Yogi Adityanath:** https://www.youtube.com/watch?v=W3NGRiTBl-0

47 **British primatologist Jane Goodall:** http://panchjanya.com/arch/2014/09/07/default.aspx

47 **"The notion of 'love jihad'":** they steal our daughters http://www.ndtv.com/opinion/the-bjp-and-hindu-muslim-romance-663589

48 **In return for converting:** http://www.business-standard.com/article/current-affairs/life-after-ghar-wapsi-in-agra-115040400659_1.html

49 **"All minorities in India have converted from Hinduism":** http://www.newindianexpress.com/thesundaystandard/VHP-Claims-Huge-Success-in-Ghar-Wapsi-Campaign/2015/07/05/article2902434.ece

50 **Selling or possessing beef:** http://indianexpress.com/article/india/india-others/beef-banned-in-maharashtra-5-yrs-jail-rs10000-fine-for-possession-or-sale/

51 **"The precise alchemy":** https://www.theguardian.com/us-news/2015/jul/01/gary-younge-farewell-to-america

56 **escaped on the waiting motorcycle:** http://www.bbc.com/news/world-asia-india-34105187

57 **"You will meet the fate of Dhabolkar":** http://indianexpress.com/article/opinion/columns/who-killed-govind-pansare/

59 **"The Unmaking of India":** http://www.ndtv.com/india-news/writer-nayantara-sahgal-returns-sahitya-akademi-award-1228565

60 **"Kashmir is ours, all of it!"** http://www.huffingtonpost.in/2016/02/15/jnu-arrest_n_9233910.html

61 "He is the 'Nation' personified":** http://gulfnews.com/opinion/thinkers/nightly-tyranny-on-india-s-small-screen-1.1468547

58 "You are more dangerous for this country than Maoist terrorists!"** https://www.youtube.com/watch?v=JIIhPFV1K28

63 a fake Twitter handle:** http://indianexpress.com/article/india/india-news-india/jnu-row-behind-govt-claim-a-fake-hafiz-saeed-tweet/

64 News X, a struggling network:** https://www.youtube.com/watch?v=XRFMi6O_8bI

68 "Comrades, my name is Umar Khalid but I am not a terrorist":** http://scroll.in/article/803988/full-text-my-name-is-umar-khalid-certainly-but-i-am-not-a-terrorist

72 A medical examination disproved his charges:** http://www.thehindu.com/news/cities/Hyderabad/abvp-leader-susheel-kumar-medical-examination-no-blunt-trauma-says-doctor/article8141788.ece

74 "Supply a nice rope":** http://raiot.in/please-serve-10mg-sodium-azide-to-all-the-dalit-students-at-the-time-of-admission/

75 "I always wanted to be

a writer":** http://raiot.in/last-words-of-rohith-vemula/

76 "There has been a malicious attempt":** http://indiatoday.intoday.in/story/rohith-vemulas-suicide-not-due-to-dalit-vs-non-dalit-confrontation-says-smriti-irani/1/575095.html

76 "No one allowed a doctor":** http://indiatoday.intoday.in/story/here-is-the-full-text-of-smriti-iranis-lok-sabha-speech-on-rohith-vemula-and-jnu-row/1/604620.html

80 "a piece of towel or something like it":** ed. Francis Robinson, *The Cambridge Illustrated History of the Islamic World*, Cambridge University Press, 1996, p. xix.

86 "less a victory of Islam":** Omer Taspinar, "The Old Turks' Revolt," *Foreign Affairs, November/December 2007.*

87 deported to a labor camp:** Kerem Karaosmanoglu, "Reimagining Minorities in Turkey," *Insight Turkey*, Vol. 2, 2010, pp. 193-212.

92 Necdet Adalı:** http://www.akparti.org.tr/english/haberler/ak-party-group-meeting-july-20-2010/25719#1

97 A confidential 2009 cable:** https://wikileaks.org/plusd/cables/09ANKARA1722_a.html

170   102   *The Plot Against the Generals:* http://drodrik.scholar.harvard.edu/files/dani-rodrik/files/plot-against-the-generals.pdf

108   **famed Turkish novelist Orhan Pamuk:** https://newrepublic.com/article/113948/orhan-pamuk-interview-taksim-square-erdogan-literature

109   **"that an elected government":** Jenny White, *Muslim Nationalism and the New Turks*, Princeton University Press, 2014.

111   **Erdoğan himself should resign:** http://www.al-monitor.com/pulse/originals/2013/12/turkey-erdogan-resignation-ministers-akp-power-corruption.html#ixzz4Bur252Uk

113   **"forming and leading a terrorist organization":** http://edition.cnn.com/2014/12/14/world/europe/turkey-media-crackdown/

115   **About 1,900 people have been charged:** http://www.bbc.com/news/world-europe-32302697

115   **50 percent of the requests Twitter received:** https://transparency.twitter.com/removal-requests/2015/jan-jun

120   **meeting between three Kurdish parliamentarians and Öcalan:** http://www.al-monitor.com/pulse/originals/2013/03/erdogan-ocalan-gulen-turkey-pkk-peace-process-presidency.html#ixzz4C8Mvzld3

120   **"We won't let you be elected president":** http://bianet.org/english/politics/163078-hdp-leader-s-one-sentence-speech-pledges-erdogan-won-t-be-the-president

126   **"For whoever wants to make life unbearable":** http://www.reuters.com/article/us-turkey-politics-presidency-idUSKCN0ST0Y120151104

136   **"They rained such intense destruction on the town":** https://www.hrw.org/sites/default/files/reports/TURKEY933.PDF

139   **"The trenches they dug have become their graves":** http://www.dw.com/en/spread-of-violence-in-turkey-shows-no-sign-of-abating/a-19320797

140   **"Hey, you so-called intellectuals!"** http://www.hurriyetdailynews.com/erdogan-slams-academics-over-petition-invites-chomsky-to-turkey.aspx?PageID=238&NID=93760&NewsCatID=338

151   **"Not a single person has come to give condolences":** https://www.theguardian.com/world/2016/jul/29/turkey-drops-cases-of-insult-against-president-in-coup-aftermath

160   **"The window was blown to pieces":** http://www.nytimes.com/2016/07/25/opinion/kashmir-and-the-inheritance-of-loss.html

Columbia Global Reports is a publishing imprint from Columbia University that commissions authors to do original on-site reporting around the globe on a wide range of issues. The resulting novella-length books offer new ways to look at and understand the world that can be read in a few hours. Most readers are curious and busy. Our books are for them.

globalreports.columbia.edu